Christmas

1991

O, star of wonder, star of night,
Star of royal beauty bright,
Westward leading, still proceeding,
Guide us to Thy perfect light.

Meredith® Press
New York, N.Y.

FOR MEREDITH® PRESS

Vice President and Editorial Director: Elizabeth P. Rice
Editiorial Project Manager: Maryanne Bannon
Project Editor: Dina von Zweck
Contributing Editors: Diane Hodges (Recipes)
                      Cyndi Marsico (Crafts)
Proofreader: G. B. Anderau
Production (Film and Separations): Bill Rose
Design: Remo Cosentino/Bookgraphics
Cover Photo: Schecter Lee
Assistants: Valerie Martone and Linda Smith

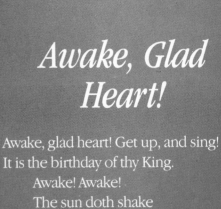

Awake, Glad Heart!

Awake, glad heart! Get up, and sing!
It is the birthday of thy King.
    Awake! Awake!
    The sun doth shake
Light from his locks, and all the way
Breathing perfumes, doth spice the day.

I would I were some bird, or star,
Fluttering in woods, or lifted far
    Above this inn
    And road of sin!
Then either star, or bird, should be
Shining, or singing, still to Thee.

HENRY VAUGHAN (1650)

Table of Contents

Christmas Miracle of Love

Christmas Wonder and Promise

Christmas With Joyful Celebration

Christmas

Miracle of Love

Christmas Lights

The Star of Bethlehem shines over the city, welcoming visitors from afar. The largest display of its kind in the world, the star is 81 feet high and 53 feet wide and is visible 20 miles to the north of Bethlehem, Pa.

Washington, D.C. Cascading lights twinkle on the White House lawn.

Salt Lake City, Utah is decked out in its festive best all through the Christmas season.

Opposite page: Crossroads Village in Flint, Michigan is ablaze with splendid holiday lights.

The St. Lucia Festival in Lindsborg, Kansas honors a Swedish saint.

Colorful ornaments enliven a holiday scene in Pierre, South Dakota.

Each Christmas season, the American Rose Center in Shreveport, Louisiana becomes a fantasy of lights.

Storrowton Village Museum in West Springfield, Massachusetts hosts a winter holiday festival during the first week of December.

Christmas lights twinkle below the radiance of the moon rising over Town Hall in Walpole, Massachusetts.

The spectacular Christmas lights on the Kearney County Courthouse in Minden, Nebraska can be seen for miles and have been a source of pride for the community and state since 1915.

Meet Me in the City

When Christmas comes to the city, same as everywhere, some of us do some peculiar things. One year I sent a Christmas card to a shopkeeper. But first let me explain...

You see, New York City is really a large collection of small villages. We reside in tiny territories with boundaries shaped by the shops, churches, schools, cafés and movie houses that we frequent. It doesn't take long to recognize the face behind the counter at the dry cleaner's and the open-til-midnight deli. Soon the news vendor by the subway is saying "Hi," and after a while, the florist throws in an extra stem or two. We're not overly friendly with one another, but I think in our little city-spheres, familiarity breeds *contentment*.

When I lived in another part of the city, however, there was one shopkeeper who was not only unfriendly, he was downright mean. He sold lumber (I was always building bookshelves and things in those days), and he'd cut it to exact sizes. He never looked at me when I'd present my order and any replies were always curt. He'd grunt and grimace and act as if he were doing me a big favor. I didn't like going in there, but his was the only lumber shop in the neighborhood.

To this day I cannot tell you specifically why, but one year as Christmas approached, I sent him a Christmas card. (And something you should know about me—I *never* send Christmas cards.) "Thank you for the good lumber you sold me this year," I wrote on it. Then mailed it and promptly forgot about it.

Months later I needed to go to the lumber loft again. I guess I shouldn't have been surprised—the man was the same: Cold. Not a word was said and again he didn't look at me. I watched him draw a two-by-four from the stacks, cut it and tie the pieces together. Then he took my money and gave me my receipt. I was almost out the door when I heard, "Mr. Varner..."

I turned, startled to hear my name. The shopkeeper was standing by his cutting machine. This time he was looking straight at me. At last he spoke.

"Come again," he said softly.

Didn't I say we do peculiar things at Christmas? We seek out relatives who bore us. We spend money we do not have. We send cards to people we don't like. Why? Because we are not ourselves at Christmas. It is one brief time when we become what we want to be, but are too busy or too stingy or too embarrassed to be the rest of the year: sentimental, forgiving, forbearing, generous, overgenerous, thoughtful, appreciative of others.

Jesus came, He said, that we might have life and have it more abundantly. And this is so at Christmas, the anniversary of His birth, when in some beautiful, mysterious way, we live beyond ourselves.

VAN VARNER

13

If We Had Been There

There are some of us ... who think to ourselves,
"If I had only been there! How quick I would have been
to help the Baby. I would have washed His linen.
How happy I would have been to go
with the shepherds to see the Lord lying in the manger!"
Yes, we would. We say that because we know
how great Christ is, but if we had been there at that time,
we would have done no better than the people of Bethlehem....
Why don't we do it now?
We have Christ in our neighbor.

MARTIN LUTHER

What Does Johnny Want?

Dear Santa Claus:
I don't want a thing that girls would like;
I don't want a velocipede, but a bike;
I don't want a gun that will not shoot;
I don't want an engine that won't toot;
I don't want mittens for the snow;
I don't want a horse-car that won't go;
I don't want anything to wear;
I don't want an apple or a pear;
I don't want anything made of tin;
I don't want a top that will not spin;
I don't want any book I can't use;
I don't want a best pair of shoes;
I don't want a ship that won't sail;
I don't want a goody-goody tale;
I don't want a game that I can't play;
I don't want a donkey that won't bray;
I don't want a small fish pond like Fred's;
I don't want one of those baby sleds;
I don't want paints that are no good;
I don't want building-blocks of wood;
I don't want *you* to think *I* am queer;
Nor I don't want you to think I don't want
  anything this year.

  Yours truly,
  Johnny.

P.S. — I was just about not to say,
I don't want you to forget me Christmas Day.

MONTROSE J. MOSES

The Symbol And The Saint

Once upon a time, a young, handsome man named Norss prepared himself for a voyage.

"Where are you going?" asked his neighbor Jans, the village blacksmith.

"I am off to search for a wife," said Norss.

"For a wife indeed!" cried Jans. "And why do you go to seek her in foreign lands? Aren't our maidens good enough?"

Then Norss said, "A spirit came to me in my dreams last night and said, 'Launch the boat and set sail tomorrow. Have no fear for I will guide you to the bride that awaits you.' Then standing, all white and beautiful, the spirit showed Norss a symbol—such as he had never seen before—in the shape of a cross, and the spirit said: 'By this symbol shall she be known to you.'"

"If this is true, you must go," said Jans. "But are you well supplied? Come to my cabin and let me give you some venison and bear's meat."

Norss shook his head. "The spirit will provide," he said. And so Norss pushed his boat down the beach into the sea, lept into the boat, and unfurled the sail to the wind. For many days he sailed. In this time, he knew no hunger or thirst. It passed as the spirit said it would: no cares or dangers troubled him. By day, the dolphins and other creatures of the sea played about his boat and kept him company; by night, a beautiful Star directed his course. And when Norss slept, he always saw the spirit dressed in white and holding the symbol of the cross before him.

At last, he came to a strange country in the Orient. The wind that filled his sail and brushed his tanned cheeks was heavy and hot with the odor of cinnamon and spices. The waters were calm and blue—very different from the white and angry waves of Norss' native fiord.

As if guided by an unseen hand, the boat pointed straight for the beach of this beautiful land. On the shore, Norss saw a maiden, shading her eyes with her right hand, and gazing intently at him. She was the most

beautiful maiden he had ever seen. Around her neck, she wore a golden chain which suspended a small symbol, which Norss didn't immediately recognize.

"Are you sailing out of the North into the East?" asked the maiden.

"Yes," said Norss.

"And you *are* Norss?" she asked.

"I am Norss. And I come seeking my bride," he answered.

"I am she," said the maiden. "My name is Faia. An angel came to me in my dreams last night, and the angel said: 'Stand upon the beach today, and Norss shall come out of the North and take you home to be his bride.'"

Remembering the spirit's words, Norss said, "What

symbol are you wearing, Faia, that I may know it is you who has spoken?"

"No symbol, but this," said Faia, holding out the gold chain. Norss looked upon the cross and knew it was the symbol of his dreams.

Norss clasped Faia in his arms and kissed her, and they entered into the boat and sailed away to the North. In all their voyage, neither care nor danger troubled them. The Star which before had led Norss into the East, now shone bright and beautiful in the Northern sky!

When Norss and his bride reached their home, Jans, the blacksmith, and the other neighbors were joyous, and all said that Faia was more beautiful than any other maiden in the land. So, Norss and Faia were wed, and went to live in the cabin in the fir-grove.

To these two was born in good time a son, whom they named Claus. On the night he was born, a wondrous thing came to pass. To the cabin in the fir-grove, all the quaint, weird spirits came: the fairies, the elves, the trolls, the pixies, the goblins, the moss-people, the gnomes, the dwarfs, the water-sprites, the brownies, the stille-volk—all came and sang the strange, beautiful songs of the Mist-Land. Full of music was that happy night.

Even in infancy, Claus did marvellous things. With his baby hands, he made pretty figures from the willows that were given to him. As he grew older, he carved many curious toys using the knife old Jans had made for him: carts, horses, dogs, houses, cats and birds—all of wood and very life-like. His mother taught him how to make dolls—dolls of every kind: baby

dolls, boy dolls, girl dolls, wax dolls, rubber dolls, paper dolls and rag dolls.

So, as you might expect, Claus became very popular with all the little boys and girls of his village. He was also very generous, and gave away all these pretty things as quickly as he made them.

Claus seemed to know by instinct every language. As he grew older he would ramble off into the woods and talk with the trees, the rocks, and the beasts of the greenwood; or he would sit on the cliffs overlooking the fiord, and listen to the stories that the waves of the sea loved to tell him; then, too, he knew the haunts of the elves and the stille-volk, and many a pretty tale he learned from these little people. When night came, old Jans told him the quaint legends of the North, and his mother sang to him the lullabies she had heard when a little child herself in the far-distant East. And every night his mother held out to him the symbol of the cross, and bade him kiss it before he went to sleep.

As Claus grew to manhood, he grew in wisdom and knowledge. His works increased too. And everywhere, he gave away all the beautiful things he created. Jans, however, being a very old man, and having no son of his own, gave Claus his forge and workshop. Claus was elated; and many, many times the Northern sky glowed with the flames that danced from the forge while Claus molded his pretty toys. And he continued to give his toys away. So little children everywhere loved Claus, and their parents also loved him because he made their little ones so happy.

But now, Norss and Faia had reached old age. After many long years of love and happiness, they knew that death was not far away. And one day Faia said to Norss: "Neither you nor I, dear love, fear death; but if we could choose, wouldn't we choose to live always in our son Claus, who has been such a sweet joy to us?"

"Yes," said Norss, "but how is that possible?"

"We shall see," said Faia.

That night, Norss dreamed that a spirit came to him, and that the spirit said to him: "Norss, you shall surely live forever in your son Claus, if you only acknowledge the symbol of the cross."

In the morning, Norss told his dream to Faia, and she said, "I had the same dream. An angel appeared to me and spoke these very words."

"But what of the symbol?" cried Norss.

"I have it here around my neck," said Faia. She then withdrew from her bosom a cross suspended from a golden chain. As she stood there, Norss thought of the time when he first saw Faia on the far-distant Orient shore, standing beneath the Star in all her maidenly glory, shading her beautiful eyes with one hand, and with the other, clasping the cross—the holy talisman of her faith.

"Faia, Faia!" cried Norss, "It is the same—the same you wore when I fetched you as a bride from the East!"

"It is the same," said Faia, "yet see how my kisses and my prayers have worn it away. For many, many times in these years, dear Norss, have I pressed it to my lips and breathed your name upon it. See now—what a beautiful light its shadow makes upon your aged face!"

And indeed, the sunbeams, streaming through the window at this moment, cast a shadow of the symbol upon Norss' brow. Norss felt a glorious warmth suffuse him, his heart lept with joy, and he stretched out his arms and fell about Faia's neck, and kissed the symbol and acknowledged it. Then Faia did the same thing. Suddenly, the place was filled with a wondrous and strange music. And from then on, Norss and Faia were never seen again.

Until late that night, Claus toiled at his forge, for it was a busy season, and he had many, many curious and beautiful things to make for all the little children in the country. The colored flames leaped singing from his forge, so that the Northern sky seemed lit by a thousand rainbows. Above all this glory, the Star beamed bright and beautiful and serene.

Coming late into the cabin in the fir-grove, Claus wondered why there was no sign of his father or mother. "Father, mother!" he cried. But there was no answer. Just then, the Star cast its golden gleam through the latticed window, and this strange, holy light fell and rested upon the symbol of the cross that lay upon the floor. Seeing it, Claus stopped and picked it up, and kissing it reverently, he cried, "Dear talisman, be my inspiration forever. And where your influence is felt, let my works be known forever!"

No sooner had he said these words, when Claus felt the gift of immortality bestowed upon him. And in that moment, too, came a knowledge that his parents'

prayer had been answered, and that Norss and Faia would live in him through all time.

And lo! To that place and in that hour came all the people of the Mist-Land and Dream-Land to declare allegiance to Claus. All the elves, the pixies, the fairies—all came to Claus, prepared to do his bidding. Joyously they played about him, and merrily they sang.

"Now make haste." cried Claus. "Make haste to your homes and bring to my workshop the best you have. Search, little hill-people, deep in the bowels of the earth for the finest gold and the choicest jewels. Fetch me, O mermaids, from the bottom of the sea the treasures hidden there. Go, pixies and other water-sprites to your secret lakes and bring the pearls! Speed! Speed you all! For we have many pretty things to make for the little ones of the earth we love.

But to the kobolds and the brownies Clause said, "Fly to every house on Earth where the cross is known. Loiter unseen in the corners, and watch and hear the children throughout the day. Keep a strict account of good and bad, and every night, bring back to me the names of good and bad, that I may know them."

The kobolds and the brownies squealed gleefully, and sped away on noiseless wings. And so too did the other fairies and elves. There also came to Claus the beasts of the forest and the birds of the sky, and asked Claus to be their master. And up danced the Four Winds, and they said, "May we not serve you too?"

The Snow-King also came in his feathery chariot. "O ho!" he cried, "I shall speed over all the world and tell them you are coming. In town and country, on the mountain tops and in the valleys—wherever the cross is raised—there will I herald your approach and there will I throw you a pathway of feathery white. O ho!" So, singing, the Snow-King stole upon his way.

But of all the beasts that begged to do him service, Claus liked the reindeer best. "You shall go with me in my travels; for I shall bear my treasures not only to the children to the North, but to the children in every land where the Star points me and where the cross is lifted up!" The reindeer neighed joyously and stamped their hoofs impatiently, as if they longed to start immediately.

Oh, many, many times Claus whirled away from his Northern home in his red sled drawn by the reindeer. He carried thousands upon thousands of beautiful gifts that he had made to the children of every land, for he loves them all the same, and of course, the children all love Claus. So truly did they love him, that they called him Santa—for I am sure he must be a Saint—Claus. He has lived many hundreds of years; and we know that since he was born of Faith and Love, he will indeed live forever.

EUGENE FIELD
Adapted by G.B. Anderau

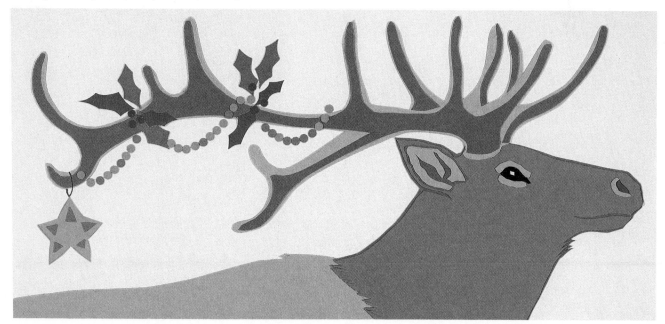

"In Excelsis Gloria!"

When Christ was born of Mary free,
In Bethlehem, in that fair citie,
Angels sang there with mirth and glee,
    In Excelsis Gloria!

Herdsmen beheld these angels bright,
To them appearing with great light,
Who said, "God's Son is born this night,"
    In Excelsis Gloria!

This King is come to save mankind,
As in Scripture truths we find,
Therefore this song have we in mind,
    In Excelsis Gloria!

Then, dear Lord, for Thy great grace,
Grant us the bliss to see Thy face,
That we may sing to Thy solace,
    In Excelsis Gloria!

OLD ENGLISH SONG (circa 1500)

Christmas Closes A Gulf

It was the Christmas after my aunt had left the house, and since it was she who always supplied the tree and the presents for my brother and myself, this first Christmas without her was a bleak and empty one. I remember that I was more or less reconciled to it, because my father had worked only spasmodically throughout the year. Two of our rooms were vacant of boarders and my mother was doing her marketing farther and farther away from our neighborhood. This was always a sign that we were dangerously close to rock bottom, and each time it occurred I came to dread it more. It was one of the vicious landmarks of poverty that I had come to know well and the one I hated most...

Obviously Christmas was out of the question—we

were barely staying alive. On Christmas Eve my father was very silent during the evening meal. Then he surprised and startled me by turning to me and saying, "Let's take a walk." He had never suggested such a thing before, and moreover, it was a very cold winter's night. I was even more surprised when he said as we left the house, "Let's go down to One Hundred Forty-ninth Street and Westchester Avenue." My heart leaped within me. That was the section where all the big stores were, where at Christmastime open pushcarts full of toys stood packed end-to-end for blocks at a stretch. On other Christmas Eves I had often gone there with my aunt, and from our tour of the carts she had gathered what I wanted the most. My father had known of this, and I joyously concluded that his walk could mean only one thing—he was going to buy me a Christmas present.

On the walk down I was beside myself with delight and an inner relief. It had been a bad year for me, that year of my aunt's going, and I wanted a Christmas present terribly—not a present merely, but a symbol, a token of some sort. I needed some sign from my father or mother that they knew what I was going through and cared for me as much as my aunt and my grandfather did. I am sure they were giving me what mute signs they could, but I did not see them. The idea that my father had managed a Christmas present for me in spite of everything filled me with a sudden peace and lightness of heart I had not known in months.

We hurried on, our heads bent against the wind, to the cluster of lights ahead that was 149th Street and Westchester Avenue, and those lights seemed to me the brightest lights I had ever seen. Tugging at my father's coat, I started down the line of pushcarts. There were all kinds of things I wanted, but since nothing had been said by my father about buying a present, I would merely pause before a pushcart to say, with as much control as I could muster, "Look at that chemistry set!" or, "There's a stamp album!" or, "Look at the printing press!" Each time my father would pause and ask the pushcart man the price. Then without a word we would move on to the next pushcart. Once or twice he would pick up a toy of some kind and look at it and then at me, as if to suggest this might be something I might like, but I was ten years old and a good deal beyond just a toy; my heart was set on a chemistry set

or a printing press. There they were on every pushcart we stopped at, but the price was always the same and soon I looked up and saw we were nearing the end of the line. Only two or three pushcarts remained. My father looked up, too, and I heard him jingle some coins in his pocket. In a flash I knew it all. He'd gotten together about seventy-five cents to buy me a Christmas present, and he hadn't dared to say so in case there was nothing to be had for so small a sum.

As I looked up at him I saw a look of despair and disappointment in his eyes that brought me closer to him than I had ever been in my life. I wanted to throw my arms around him and say, "It doesn't matter...I understand...this is better than a chemistry set or a printing press...I love you." But instead we stood shivering beside each other for a moment—then turned away from the last two pushcarts and started silently back home. I don't know why the words remained choked up within me. I didn't even take his hand on the way home, nor did he take mine. We were not on that basis. Nor did I ever tell him how close to him I felt that night—that for a little while the concrete wall between father and son had crumbled away and I knew that we were two lonely people struggling to reach each other.

I came close to telling him many years later, but again the moment passed. Again it was Christmas and I was on my way to visit him in Florida. My father was a bright and blooming ninety-one years of age now and I arrived in Florida with my wife to spend Christmas and New Year's with him. On Christmas Eve we sat in his living room, and while my wife chatted with his nurse and companion, I sat on a sofa across the room with my father, showing him the pictures of his two grandchildren. Suddenly I felt his hand slip into mine. It was the first time in our lives that either of us had ever touched the other. No words were spoken and I went right on turning the pages of the picture album, but my hand remained over his. A few years before I might have withdrawn mine after a moment or two, but now my hand remained; nor did I tell him what I was thinking and feeling. The moment was enough. It had taken forty years for the gulf that separated us to close.

MOSS HART

25

Christmas

Wonder and Promise

The Christmas Day Heart

Let me be glad again a little while,
    and see the world all hung with tinsel chains,
Hear reindeer hoofs and see old Santa smile
    through every window's frost-embroidered panes.

Let me unwrap the years and, one by one,
    find each wrapper brighter and more gay,
Till suddenly the gist and goal are won —
    and I unwrap my child's heart stored away.

Let me unwrap the heart that long ago
    beat like a silver bell when morning came,
Hearing the wakened folk move to and fro
    and the big fireplace snap in roaring flame.

Let me unwrap the heart that seemed to climb
    into my throat and throb there mightily
Waiting for father to say: "Now's the time!"
    back flung the doors and bloomed
        the Christmas tree.

Let me unwrap the heart that knew no doubt
    of the great North Pole castle, where all year
Old Santa wrought the toys and trinkets out
    that piled before our raptured vision here.

Let me unwrap the heart that listened well
    to mother singing, and to mother's voice
Tuned with the old reed organ's notes to tell
    how angels came and bade the world rejoice.

Let me unwrap the heart that simply knelt
    with all the rest among the gifts to pray
And stammer out the thanks it truly felt
    unto the One who gave us Christmas Day.

Let me unwrap a heart that leaps in tune
    with that of my own child; a heart that lifts
The same fresh song of joy I hear her croon
as we kneel, rapt, among our Christmas gifts.

DEAN COLLINS

Trumpeting Angel

· ·

This charming wooden angel is sanded to make it look weathered, and then painted to give it a folkloric look. Display your handiwork on a wall next to your dining table or on a mantel festooned with fragrant pine boughs. What better way to announce the joys of the Christmas season?

SIZE

Angel, about 12″ wide.

EQUIPMENT

Pencil. Ruler. Tracing paper. Carbon paper. Strong clamp or vise. Hack saw. Fret saw. Screw driver. Medium- and fine-grade sandpaper. Thin dowel. Flat and round sanding blocks. Tack cloth. Sable brushes, large and fine, for acrylic paint. Wide, flat brushes, for oil paint and varnish. Tiny stencil brush. Toothbrush. Linseed oil, artist quality. Clean, dry cloths. Paper towels.

MATERIALS

Pine, planed and ready for use, ¾″ thick, piece 13″x16″. Acrylic paints: tomato red, light blue, mustard, brown, black, flesh color, and ivory. Raw umber oil paint. Matte varnish (optional).

DIRECTIONS

To Cut Out Angel: Trace actual-size angel pattern, matching lines of design to make complete pattern. Transfer heavy lines (cutting lines) to wood, using carbon paper and pencil; use ruler to mark straight lines, such as underside of gown and boot bottoms.

Secure marked wood in place on table, using clamp or vise. Cut straight lines with hack saw. Use fret saw for curves. Saw through hand as shown for ease in cutting away opening below chin. Use screw driver to gouge scratches in wood, working as desired along straight grain of wood, for weathered effect; do not gouge face.

Sand all wood surfaces and edges, using flat and rounded sanding blocks as necessary. Use sandpaper wrapped around a pencil or dowel for cutout and other fine curves. Dust wood with tack cloth.

To Paint: Transfer fine lines (painting lines) to angel; do not mark facial features until directed.

Paint individual areas of angel as directed below; extend paint to side edges of wood. Mix paints as necessary to achieve desired colors (see color photograph); add ivory to achieve lighter shades; add black or brown for darker shades. Rinse brushes thoroughly and allow paint to dry between color changes.

Gown: Paint basecoat with light blue. Paint topcoat with red. Highlight waist.

Boots and hair: Paint basecoat with brown or red. Paint topcoat with black.

Wing: Paint basecoat with mustard. Paint topcoat with ivory.

Face and hand: Paint with two coats flesh color. Add shading on hand with light brown.

Horn: Paint basecoat with flesh color. Paint topcoat with mustard. Add shading above and below hands with brown and dark brown.

Facial features: When all other painting is completed, transfer and paint facial features (see Face Diagram), using very fine brushes: Outline eyebrow and nostril with black, eye and lashes with brown. Paint pupil with brown, iris with black. Add white of eye and "sparkle" with ivory. Outline lips with reddish brown; fill with red; highlight with flesh color. Add shading to hairline and neck edge with light brown.

Use tiny stencil brush and red-

dish brown to paint cheek: Dip brush into paint; tap bristles on paper towel until brush is almost dry, then apply color to cheek, using bristle tips and a circular motion; repeat until desired depth of color is achieved; do not fill in cheek solidly.

To "Age": Mix brown and black paints to make very dark brown; paint should have the consistency of egg whites. Cover angel's face and hand to protect from paint. Use toothbrush and dark brown to add tiny splattered dots to selected areas of gown and horn; practice technique as necessary on scrap

paper before dotting angel. To splatter, put small amount of paint on brush; rub finger or pencil across bristles to splatter paint for desired effect; let dry.

Sand painted surfaces of angel in a random manner, working on selected areas to give the appearance of weathering; do not sand face or hand. Sand some areas down to basecoat; see photograph. Dust with tack cloth.

Use wide brush to apply burnt umber oil paint to cover angel completely, so that paint gets into all cracks and scratches on wood. Immediately begin to remove oil paint, using clean cloth and a circu-

lar motion to randomly wipe away more or less paint in individual areas as desired. (Note: If you are not satisfied with results of this step, you can clean off all oil paint with linseed oil and begin again; linseed oil will not affect acrylics.) Let dry, at least 48 hours.

To Finish: If desired, seal all surfaces of angel with matte varnish, following manufacturer's directions. Let dry. Mount hanger on back of wood, for displaying angel on wall, or display on flat surface, such as a table or mantle.

Designed by MARINA GRANT

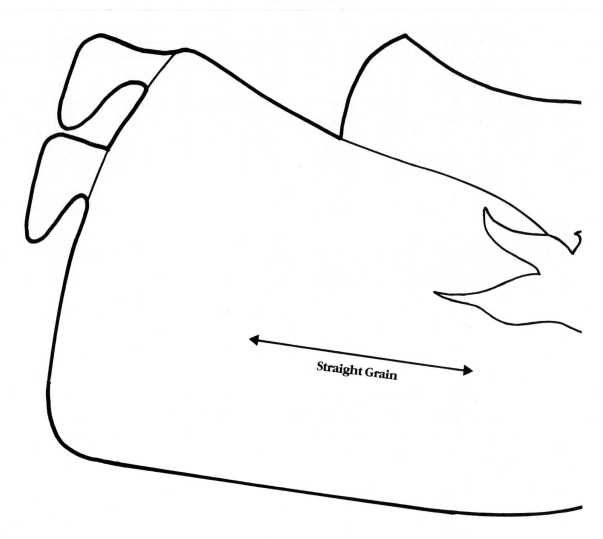

Straight Grain

Face Diagram

An Exchange of Gifts

I grew up believing that Christmas was a time when strange and wonderful things happened, when wise and royal visitors came riding, when at midnight the barnyard animals talked to one another, and in the light of a fabulous star God came down to us as a little Child. Christmas to me has always been a time of enchantment, and never more so than the year that my son Marty was eight.

That was the year that my children and I moved into a cozy trailer home in a forested area just outside of Redmond, Washington. As the holiday approached, our spirits were light, not to be dampened even by the winter rains that swept down Puget Sound to douse our home and make our floors muddy.

Throughout that December Marty had been the most spirited, and busiest, of us all. He was my youngest, a cheerful boy, blond-haired and playful, with a quaint habit of looking up at you and cocking his head like a puppy when you talked to him. Actually the reason for this was that Marty was deaf in his left ear, but it was a condition that he never complained about.

For weeks I'd been watching Marty. I knew that something was going on with him that he was not telling me about. I saw how *eagerly* he made his bed, took out the trash, and *carefully* set the table and helped Rick and Pam prepare dinner before I got home from work. I saw how he silently collected his tiny allowance and tucked it away, spending not a cent of it. I had no idea what all this quiet activity was about, but I suspected that somehow it had something to do with Kenny.

Kenny was Marty's friend, and ever since they'd found each other in the springtime, they were seldom apart. If you called to one, you got them both. Their world was in the meadow, a horse pasture broken by a small winding stream, where the boys caught frogs and snakes, where they'd search for arrowheads or hidden treasure, or where they'd spend an afternoon feeding peanuts to the squirrels.

Times were hard for our little family, and we had to do some scrimping to get by. With my job as a meat wrapper and with a lot of ingenuity around the trailer, we managed to have elegance on a shoestring. But not Kenny's family. They were desperately poor, and his mother was having a real struggle to feed and clothe her two children. They were a good, solid family; but Kenny's mom was a proud woman, very proud, and she had strict rules.

How we worked, as we did each year, to make our home festive for the holiday! Ours was a handcrafted Christmas of gifts hidden away and ornaments strung about the place.

Marty and Kenny would sometimes sit still at the table long enough to help make cornucopias or weave little baskets for the tree; but then, in a flash, one would whisper to the other, and they would be out the door and sliding cautiously under the electric fence into the horse pasture that separated our home from Kenny's.

One night shortly before Christmas, when my hands were deep in *peppernöder* dough, shaping tiny nutlike Danish cookies heavily spiced with cinnamon, Marty came to me and said in a tone mixed with pleasure and pride, "Mom, I've bought Kenny a Christmas present. Want to see it?" *So that's what he's been up to,* I said to myself. "It's something he's wanted for a long, long time, Mom."

After carefully wiping his hands on a dish towel, he pulled from his pocket a small box. Lifting the lid, I gazed at the pocket compass that my son had been saving all those allowances to buy. A little compass to point an eight-year-old adventurer through the woods.

"It's a lovely gift, Martin," I said, but even as I spoke, a disturbing thought came to mind. I knew how Kenny's mother felt about their poverty. They could barely afford to exchange gifts among themselves, and giving presents to others was out of the question. I was sure that Kenny's proud mother would not permit her son to receive something he could not return in kind.

Gently, carefully, I talked over the problem with Marty. He understood what I was saying.

"I know, Mom, *I know*...but what if it was a *secret?* What if they never found out *who* gave it?"

I didn't know how to answer him. I just didn't know.

The day before Christmas was rainy and cold and gray. The three kids and I all but fell over one another as we elbowed our way about our little home, putting finishing touches on Christmas secrets and preparing for family and friends who would be dropping by.

Night settled in. The rain continued. I looked out the window over the sink and felt an odd sadness. How mundane the rain seemed for a Christmas Eve. Would wise and royal men come riding on such a night? I doubted it. It seemed to me that strange and wonderful things happened only on clear nights, nights when one could at least see a star in the heavens.

I turned from the window, and as I checked on the ham and *lefse* bread warming in the oven, I saw Marty slip out the door. He wore his coat over his pajamas, and he clutched a tiny, colorfully wrapped box in his pocket.

Down through the soggy pasture he went, then a quick slide under the electric fence and across the yard to Kenny's house. Up the steps on tiptoes, shoes squishing; open the screen door just a crack; the gift placed on the doorstep; then a deep breath, a reach for the doorbell and a press on it *hard*.

Quickly Marty turned, ran down the steps and across the yard in a wild race to get away unnoticed. Then, suddenly, he banged into the electric fence.

The shock sent him reeling. He lay stunned on the wet ground. His body tingled and he gasped for breath. Then slowly, weakly, confused and frightened, he began the grueling trip back home.

"Marty," we cried as he stumbled through the door, "what happened?" His lower lip quivered, his eyes brimmed.

"I forgot about the fence, and it knocked me down!"

I hugged his muddy little body to me. He was still dazed, and there was a red mark beginning to blister on his face from his mouth to his ear. Quickly I treated the blister and, with a warm cup of cocoa soothing him, Marty's bright spirits returned. I tucked him into bed and just before he fell asleep he looked up at me and said, "Mom, Kenny didn't see me. I'm sure he didn't see me."

That Christmas Eve I went to bed unhappy and puzzled. It seemed such a cruel thing to happen to a little boy while on the purest kind of Christmas mission, doing what the Lord wants us all to do, giving to others, and giving in secret at that. I did not sleep well that night. Somewhere deep inside I think I must have been feeling the disappointment that the night of Christmas had come and it had been just an ordinary, problem-filled night, no mysterious enchantment at all.

But I was wrong.

By morning the rain had stopped and the sun shone. The streak on Marty's face was very red, but I could tell that the burn was not serious. We opened our presents, and soon, not unexpectedly, Kenny was knocking on the door, eager to show Marty his new compass and tell about the mystery of its arrival. It was plain that Kenny didn't suspect Marty at all, and while the two of them talked, Marty just smiled and smiled.

Then I noticed that while the two boys were comparing their Christmases, nodding and gesturing and chattering away, Marty was not cocking his head. When Kenny was talking, Marty seemed to be listening with his deaf ear. Weeks later a report came from the school nurse, verifying what Marty and I already knew: "Marty now has complete hearing in *both* ears."

The mystery of how Marty regained his hearing, and still has it, remains just that—a mystery. Doctors suspect, of course, that the shock from the electric fence was somehow responsible. Perhaps so. Whatever the reason, I just remain thankful to God for the good exchange of gifts that was made that night.

So you see, strange and wonderful things still happen on the night of our Lord's birth. And one does not have to have a clear night, either, to follow a fabulous star.

DIANE RAYNER

Christmas Wreaths

Oh let us wind the holly
　　In Christmas garlands gay,
It lives so long, and glistens
　　When roses fade away!

Wind it on the stairs and windows
　　And on the cradles, too —
The babies love the holly
　　Quite as much as you.

Christmas was made for babies,
　　All their own to keep;
It's the birthday of that Baby
　　Who was cradled with the sheep.

Here's holly for the babies!
　　And on their cribs upstairs
We'll weave its branches, green and
　　　　red,
　　For Christmas day is theirs.

ANDREA HOFER PROUDFOOT

Jingle Bell Wreath

*Bells and bows decorate this fanciful wreath.
It's easy-to-make...so you can make more than one
for housewarming gifts or school and church fairs.*

SIZE

Wreath, 10″ diameter, plus bells.

EQUIPMENT

Ruler. Scissors. T-pins.

MATERIALS

Styrofoam wreath with rounded edges, 10″ diameter. Red ribbon: velvet 1⅜″ wide, 4 yards; satin ⅛″ wide, 13 yards. Foil star garland, 4 yards gold/silver. Jingle bells ⅜″-¾″ diameter, 96 gold and/or silver. Straight pins with flat heads.

Velvet Ribbon: Use velvet ribbon to cover styrofoam wreath (see Wrapping Diagram): Thread one end of ribbon through wreath opening from back to front; take end up and over wreath top; pin on back to secure; make sure right side of ribbon faces out and wrong side of ribbon is against styrofoam. Wrap ribbon around wreath to cover completely, working in a clockwise direction as shown; overlap edges about ¼″; pin on back of wreath as necessary to secure ribbon and keep it flat. When wreath is completely covered, clip end behind wreath; pin to secure.

Jingle Bells: Use T-pins to mark off 8 equal sections around inner edge of wreath (Fig. 1): Divide edge in half, pushing a T-pin (A) into styrofoam at center top and bottom of wreath opening; divide and subdivide each half of edge until 8 pins have been equally spaced. Rotate wreath until two A's are at top and bottom, then use a T-pin (B) to mark center top and bottom of wreath along outer edge (Fig. 2); B's should be equally spaced between pairs of A's as shown; Divide and subdivide edge until 8 B's have been equally spaced (Fig. 3).

Cut 8′ length satin ribbon; use to thread all jingle bells through their hanging loops; arrange bells as desired, if using more than one color or size; secure one ribbon

SPECIAL HINTS

Straight pins are used to permanently anchor trims in place on wreath and are not removed after construction. Use flat-headed pins and push them straight into styrofoam until heads lie flat against wreath; keep trims and pins as smooth as possible.

T-pins are used to mark placement of trims and are removed when construction is complete. Push T-pins only halfway into styrofoam, to allow for easy removal later.

Wrapping Diagram

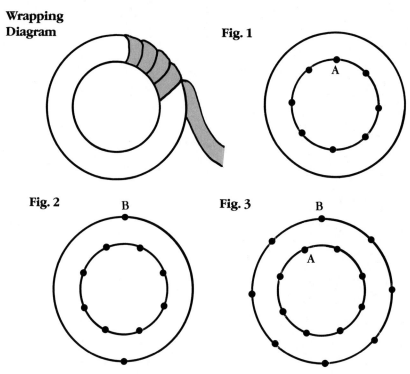

Fig. 1

Fig. 2   B

Fig. 3   B

end. Position wreath with one B at center top. Thread free ribbon end through wreath from front to back; pin securely on back, behind top. Wrap ribbon smoothly and flatly around front of wreath, along left-hand side of one top A-B pair (Fig. 4); slide 6 bells down ribbon until they lie centered along A-B line; pin ribbon at ends of 6-bell string to secure.

Working clockwise as before, wrap ribbon around wreath, coming out at left of next A-B pair and pinning on back as necessary to keep ribbon flat; slide another 6 bells down ribbon to wreath front; center along A-B line; pin ends to secure. Continue wrapping in this manner until 8 strings of bells have been threaded around wreath (Fig. 5); do not end off ribbon. Turning ribbon and changing direction, wrap wreath counterclockwise in same manner to form star pattern (Fig. 6), but working along right side of A-B pairs; clip ribbon end on back; pin to secure. Do not remove T-pins until directed.

Star Garland: Working as for satin ribbon, thread one end of garland through wreath; secure with straight pin behind wreath top; wrap garland around wreath clockwise, working along left-hand side of strings of bells, and then counterclockwise, working along right-hand side of bells (Fig. 7). Clip and secure end on wreath back.

Loopy Bows: Subdivide outer edge of wreath once more, placing 8 T-pins (C) halfway between pairs of adjacent B's (Fig. 8). Make 8 loopy bows: For each bow, cut two lengths satin ribbon, one 36″ and one 8″. Accordion-fold longer ribbon to form 3″-wide loopy bow (see Bow Diagram); tie shorter ribbon around center of bow to secure; do not clip ends. Pin bows around outer edge of wreath at C's.

When all bows are in place, carefully remove T-pins. Hang wreath as desired.

Designed by LINDA HEBERT

SPECIAL HINTS

All bells should be on front of wreath. Trims should lie as flat and smooth as possible on back so that completed wreath will lie flat against wall.

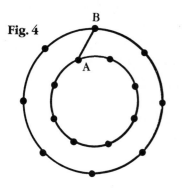

Fig. 4

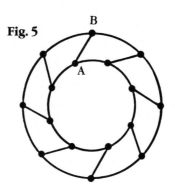

Fig. 5

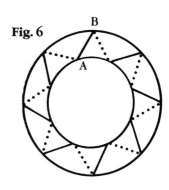

Fig. 6

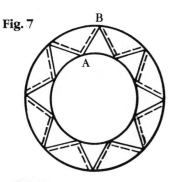

Fig. 7

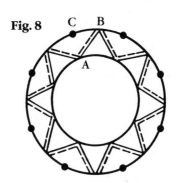

Fig. 8

Bow Diagram

Christmas Tree Centerpiece

. . . .

A delightful showpiece for your table. The tree
is decorated with favorite childhood toys —
gingerbread man, toy soldier, drum, kite,
train and other old-fashioned treasures.
Everyone will enjoy this unique addition to holiday dining.

SIZE

Tree with base, about 13½" high.

EQUIPMENT

Cookie baking sheets, three 17"x14". Pencil. Ruler. Compass. Tracing paper, lightweight cardboard, and white glue, for templates. Scissors. Masking tape. Aluminum foil. Waxed paper. Rolling pin. Clean dishclothes. Sharp paring knife. Pastry tube with #2, #3, #4, and #5 tips. Mixing bowls. Spatula. Colorfast cord or twine.

MATERIALS

Architectural Dough, Royal Icing, and Flow Icing (see recipes). Paste food coloring: red, yellow, blue, green, violet, and brown. Small round cinnamon candies. Gumdrops, about 26 each red and green. About 16 tiny gift-wrapped boxes.

Architectural Dough

- 2¼ **cups margarine or butter (4½ sticks) or solid shortening**
- 3⅜ **cups granulated or brown sugar**
- 2¼ **teaspoons salt**
- 2¼ **teaspoons baking soda**
- 10½ **teaspoons ground ginger**
- 6 **teaspoons ground cinnamon**
- 3 **teaspoons ground cloves**
- 3 **teaspoons grated nutmeg (freshly grated, if possible)**
- 1½ **teaspoons ground cardamom**
- 2¼ **cups molasses, dark or light**
- ¾ **cup water 10½–12 cups all-purpose flour (*not* Wondra or self-rising)**

In big bowl, cream margarine and sugar. Blend in salt, baking soda, and spices. Stir in molasses and water. Add 6 cups flour; mix thoroughly. Stir in remaining 6 cups flour, a cup or so at a time, until well mixed. Wrap dough tightly in plastic.

Royal Icing

- 9 **egg whites**
- 1½ **teaspoons cream of tartar**
- 3 **pounds (approximately 10½–12 cups) confectioners' sugar**
- 1½ **teaspoons orange or lemon extract (optional)**

Using grease-free utensils and bowl, mix all ingredients together on low speed of mixer for 2 minutes. Then beat 5–8 minutes more on moderately high speed until icing forms peaks with a spoon. If peaks do not form after maximum time, beat for a minute or two at a higher speed. Do not overbeat, or icing will become weak and difficult to work with. Keep icing covered with a damp cloth or tightly fitted lid.

Flow Icing

Thin Royal Icing *slightly* with water. Be careful not to thin icing too much, or it will lose its luster and look flat. Check consistency by dropping a bit from a spoon across iced surface. The drop should take about 3–4 seconds to blend in; if it blends in immediately, it is too thin; add confectioners' sugar, a tiny bit at a time, to thicken. Keep icing tightly covered when not in use.

TO MAKE TREE

Make four templates: Make tracing of actual-size patterns for right-half tree top and bottom, using ruler to mark straight side edge; move paper as necessary to draw entire tree half, lining up dash lines at lower edge of tree top and upper edge of tree bottom. Make another tracing of tree, completing half-pattern indicated by vertical dash line,

for tree with left and right halves. Make separate tracing of star pattern. For base pattern, mark 12"-diameter circle on tracing paper. Glue tracings to cardboard; let dry; cut out templates.

Make dough. Cover cookie sheets with aluminum foil. Divide dough and put one third on each cookie sheet. Roll out each to a 16"x14" rectangle, ¼" thick. (To prevent slippage during rolling, place damp cloth under cookie sheet. If dough is hard to roll, cover rolling pin with a stockinet; coat with flour.) Place sheets of dough into refrigerator to chill at least 30 minutes. Set oven to preheat at 350°. Dust templates lightly with flour. Remove sheets of dough from refrigerator.

Using sharp paring knife and leaving ½" between pieces, carefully cut around templates placed on dough, to make the following pieces: From one sheet of dough, cut two tree halves. From second sheet, cut one complete tree and star (tree-top ornament). Cut base from third sheet of dough. Remove excess dough around pieces. Bake 30–40 minutes, or until edges begin to turn brown and cookies are set. Let cool completely.

TO DECORATE

When all pieces are cool, gently remove from foil with spatula. Make Royal Icing; set ⅙ icing aside for ornaments. Decorate one surface of tree, tree-top star, and base pieces: Use white Royal Icing and #4 or #5 tip to pipe ⅛"–¼" from edges; do not pipe straight inner edges of half-trees. Use #3 tip and Flow Icing to fill base with white,

star with yellow, and tree with green. Let pieces dry thoroughly (at least 24 hours). When pieces are dry, turn tree and star cookies over onto clean dishcloths; decorate as before; do not decorate second surface (underneath) of base.

To Make Ornaments: Divide ornament icing in half. Using one half, place equal portions into six individual bowls; tint to make desired colors. Leave remainder of dough white for piping. Make toys and Royal Icing hearts and flowers as directed below, referring to color photograph. Make ornaments on waxed paper taped securely in place; let dry thoroughly (at least 24 hours) before use.

Toys: Make four tracings of each actual-size toy ornament pattern, marking all outlines and design lines except kite tail; go over lines to darken. Place tracings under waxed paper with design lines showing through. Make toys, using #2 or #3 tip, Royal Icing for piping, and Flow Icing to fill individual areas of design: With white, pipe outline and main design lines of each toy; kite tail will be piped after mounting on tree. Let piping dry. Fill in all areas solidly to prevent breaking when toys are removed from waxed paper; let dry thoroughly. When toys are dry, use Royal Icing to make additional features: Make tinted dots for eyes, mouths, and buttons; use white to re-pipe some features, such as soldier's suspenders and drum straps, for added dimension.

Royal Icing Heart: Use #3 or #4 tip and make one half of heart at a time: Hold bag at 45° angle and

make a dot on waxed paper. Relax pressure on bag and draw tip toward you, making half of a small "V." Repeat for second half of heart.

Royal Icing Flower: Use #4 or #5 tip and icing of a slightly thicker consistency (add a bit more confectioners' sugar). Make six-petaled flower, making each petal as follows: Hold bag at 90° angle with tip touching waxed paper; twist wrist to left or right. Apply pressure to bag as you untwist your wrist to form petal; stop pressing and pull bag away. When all petals are complete, add center dot of contrasting color, using #3 tip.

Remove ornaments carefully from waxed paper. Glue ornaments and cinnamon candies to both frosted surfaces of tree pieces, using Royal Icing; do not place ornaments along vertical center of either surface of whole tree. Pipe each kite tail, using white Royal Icing and #2 or #3 tip.

SPECIAL HINTS

Chilling the dough helps relax the flour's gluten and will prevent excess spreading of cookies during baking.

Scraps of Architectural Dough may be re-rolled and used to make thin cookies, 1½6"–⅛" thick.

TO ASSEMBLE

Use green Royal Icing to pipe straight edges of half-trees; press in place along vertical center of each surface of whole tree; see Assembly Diagram. Pipe a line of green along both sides of each "seam." Tie cord or twine around tree at branch indentations to secure tree during drying; let dry thoroughly; remove cord. Pipe white Royal Icing along straight bottom edges of trees; press in place, centered, on base; pipe "seams"; let dry. Glue star in place on top of tree. Glue gumdrops inside piping around edge of base, alternating red and green; let dry.

When centerpiece is thoroughly dry, arrange gift-wrapped "presents" around tree at base.

Designed by JANN JOHNSON

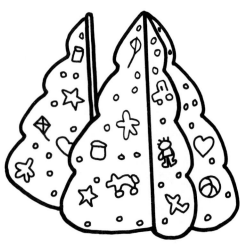

Assembly Diagram

TOY ORNAMENTS

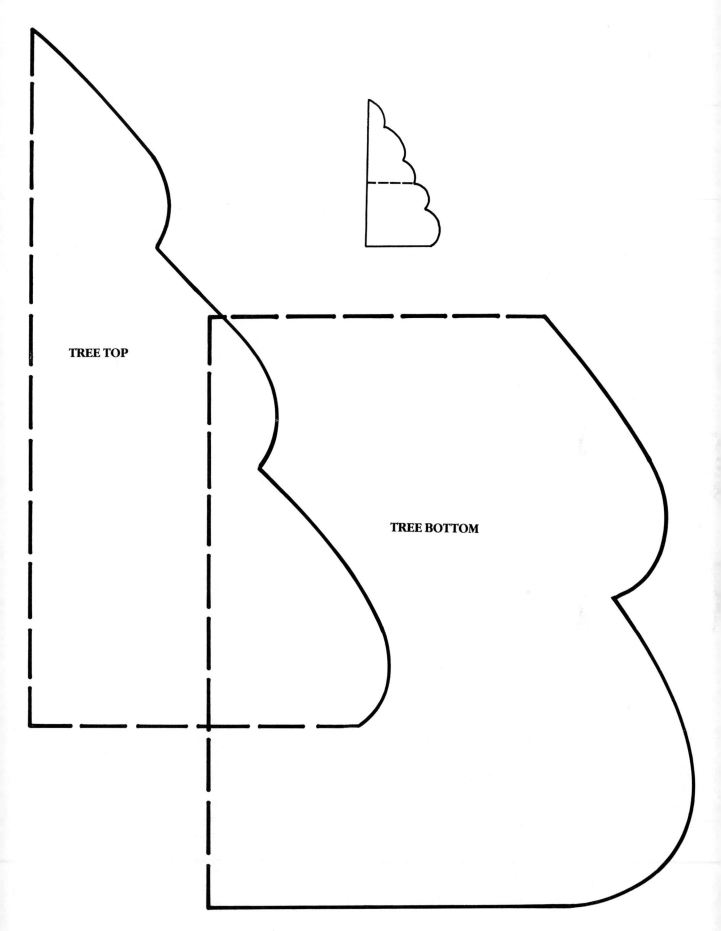

TREE TOP

TREE BOTTOM

45

One Room, One Window

Mrs. Morton was an elderly widow and a permanent tenant in the guest house where I lived in Oakland, California.

Tony was, to us, simply a sullen man who owned the rooming house next door.

Once our house had been the mansion of a California senator; now it was a sheltering stronghold for teachers, business people and retirees. Many of the dwellings on once-fashionable Jackson Street, plush landmarks of an earlier era, had become victims of age. One such was the crumbling white house in which Tony and his wife lived.

Everyone on the block agreed that Tony was unfriendly, yet we had to admit that he worked untiringly in his garden and had restored his weed-rioting premises to prideful order. In that garden there was a huge magnolia tree, a beautiful tree which Tony worshiped much as the Druids did their oak. But one large branch shadowed our house and obscured the view from the single window of Mrs. Morton's room. Many times the old lady had wished aloud that the branch were not there. "I do believe I could see Lake Merritt," she would say wistfully. The lake was only a block distant.

Tactfully, Miss Plunkett, our housekeeper, suggested to Tony that he cut off the branch. He was outraged. Even I, one courage-giving, brisk October day, hinted to Tony how dark Mrs. Morton's room was. More outrage.

Then Christmas came. That morning I accompanied Miss Plunkett on her cheery rounds of the rooms and when we visited Mrs. Morton, we found her radiantly excited. "Come see!" she said, tugging us across the room.

Her window now framed a seascape of beauty; diamonds sparkled on the rippling blue waters of Lake Merritt. The obstructing branch had been cut away.

Miss Plunkett and I hastened next door to thank Tony. I think he was happy to see us, but he shuffled with embarrassment.

"How did you come to do it?" I asked.

Tony groped for expression. "It's Christmas," he said finally.

Christmas, I thought. The old wonderful miracle had repeated itself. Hearts are gentled. Strangers, however self-serving, bring gifts of brotherhood....

"What a lovely gift," Miss Plunkett said.

"But, lady," he said, "*I* got the gift."

We did not know what he meant until, beckoning us outside, Tony pointed, with surprised joy, to his cherished tree. "Look, she's more pretty than before!"

It was true. Removing the wayward limb had destroyed none of the tree's grace. Rather, the magnolia now towered heavenward with sharpened beauty, a symmetry that truly made it the showpiece of Tony's garden, quite the grandest "Christmas tree" on our block.

EVA DUNBAR

Felt Ornaments

Bell and Tree ornaments...and Tree Top Angel are simply beautiful decorations. Embroidered designs add an extra-special note of elegance. These soft sculpture pieces are classic ornaments that always look fresh.

Felt Ornaments

SIZES

Bell, 3¼″ square.
Tree, 3¼″x4½″.

EQUIPMENT

Pencil. Ruler. Tracing paper. Dressmaker's tracing (carbon) paper. Dry ball-point pen. Scissors. Pinking shears. Embroidery needle. Straight pins.

MATERIALS

For Each Bell: Felt, two 4″ squares red or white. Six-strand embroidery floss, one skein green, plus white (for red bell) or red (for white bell). Fine gold metallic thread. Batting.

For Each Tree: Felt, two 5″ squares green. Six-strand embroidery floss, one skein red, plus small amount yellow-gold (for Star B). Fine gold metallic thread. Batting.

DIRECTIONS

Trace actual-size ornament pattern, marking heavy outline and fine embroidery lines; trace Bow for bell and Star for tree. Transfer pattern to one felt square, using dressmaker's carbon and dry ball-point pen.

Work embroidery, referring to stitch details and using three strands floss in needle or enough strands gold metallic thread to equal thickness of three strands floss.

Bell: Work holly in outline stitch with green. Work bow in satin stitch, using white on red felt, or red on white felt.

Tree: Work balls in satin stitch with red. Work garland in chain stitch, using gold metallic thread. Use gold metallic to work double cross-

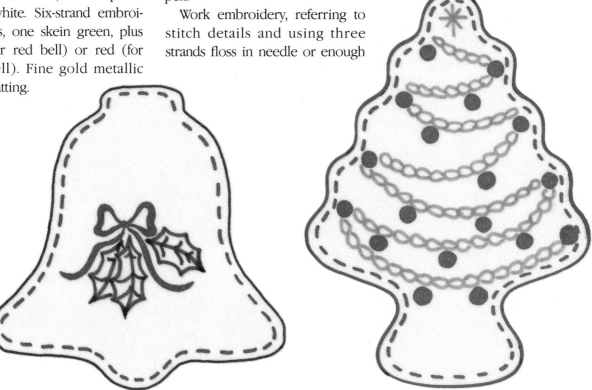

stitch Star; use yellow-gold floss to work satin stitch Star.

When all embroidery is complete, stack felt squares with embroidery face up and edges even; pin. Cut out shape along marked outline, using pinking shears and cutting through both felt layers, for embroidered ornament front and plain ornament back. Use regular scissors to cut same-size shape from thin layer batting; trim away ¼" batting all around.

To assemble ornament, center batting between felt front and back pieces (see Assembly Diagram) with embroidery face up; pin. Stitch ornament together, using three strands contrasting color floss and running stitch; make stitches ⅛" from edges, working through felt layers only.

For hanging loop, cut 6" length gold metallic thread. Thread length through ornament top; even ends and tie knot or bow.

Designed by DIANE WAGNER

FELT ORNAMENT ASSEMBLY DIAGRAM

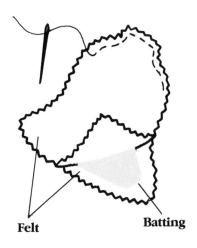

Felt   **Batting**

Tree-Top Angel
SIZE
Angel, 7¼"x5¼".

EQUIPMENT
Pencil. Ruler. Tracing paper. Dressmaker's tracing (carbon) paper. Dry ball-point pen. Scissors. Pinking shears. Embroidery and sewing needles. Straight pins.

MATERIALS
Felt: two 8" squares white; one 3" square green. Six-strand embroidery floss, one skein each pale pink, bright pink, yellow-gold, light blue, red, and green. Fine gold metallic thread. Batting.

DIRECTIONS
Trace actual-size tree-top angel pattern, marking heavy outline of angel and tree, plus fine embroidery lines on angel only. Make separate tracings of tree with stars and tree mount.

Transfer angel and mount patterns to one white felt square, using dressmaker's carbon and dry ball-point pen. Transfer tree pattern to green felt; cut out along marked outline, using pinking shears. Pin and baste tree in place between angel's hands where indicated.

Work embroidery on angel and tree, referring to stitch details and using three strands floss in needle or enough strands gold metallic thread to equal thickness of three strands floss: Use satin stitch to work angel's cheeks and hands with pale pink; work eyes with light blue. Work mouth in outline stitch with bright pink. Work hair in outline stitch with yellow-gold. Using gold metallic thread, work upper and lower edges of angel's cap in chain stitch; work starts on tree with double cross-stitches, making stitches through both felt layers; remove basting. Use outline stitch to outline wings with light blue, gown and sleeves with red. Work upper and lower wavy lines on gown bottom in green chain stitch. Work center wavy line in threaded running stitch, using green for running stitches and red for threading.

When all embroidery is complete, stack white felt squares with embroidery face up and straight edges even; pin. Cut out angel along outline, cutting through both felt layers. Cut out tree mount from marked layer only; set aside. Cut angel shape from thin layer of batting; trim away ¼" batting all around.

To assemble tree-top angel, center batting between felt front and back pieces (see Assembly Diagram) with embroidery face up; pin together. Stitch through all layers with white sewing thread and running stitch, following Fig. 1 for placement of stitches alongside embroidery lines.

To attach tree mount, pin it to wrong side of angel, following heavy outline in Fig. 2 for placement. Unpin left edge of mount and repin it along dotted line, forming a channel under felt. Whipstitch around sides and top of mount to secure.

Designed by DIANE WAGNER

STITCH DETAILS

 Satin Stitch

 **Running Stitch**

 **Chain Stitch**

 **Outline Stitch**

 Double Cross-Stitch

Threaded Running Stitch

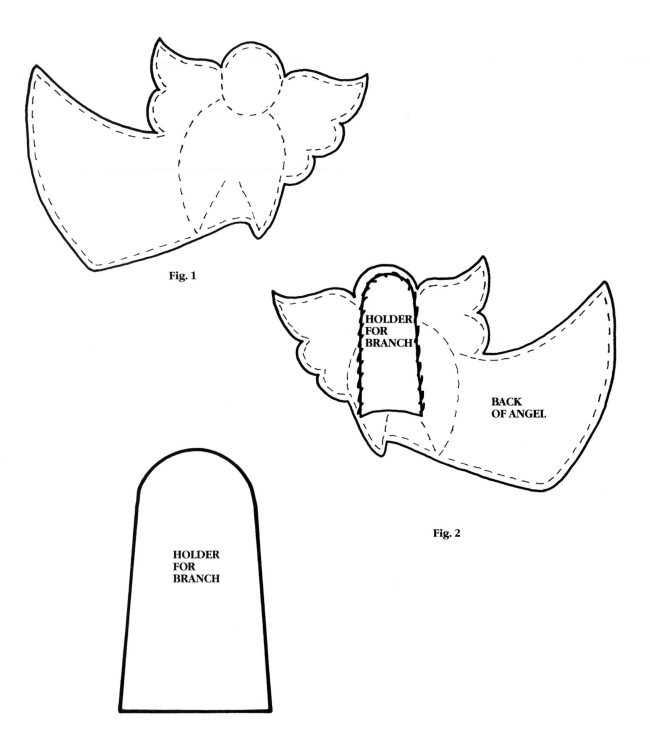

Fig. 1

HOLDER
FOR
BRANCH

BACK
OF ANGEL

Fig. 2

HOLDER
FOR
BRANCH

Frost Flowers

Fragile winter dreams in ice,
sparkling thistledown,
and frosted stars
tremble in the morning light,
melt, and freeze anew.

CANDIDA PALMER

Cross-Stitch
Angel Ornaments

. . . .

Angel, angels and more angels. Make as many as you like for the Christmas tree. Soft colors combine with metallic threads to create subdued drama.

SIZE

Each ornament, 3¼"x5½".

EQUIPMENT

Pencil. Ruler. Scissors. Masking tape (optional). Tracing paper, light-weight cardboard, and white glue, for template. Embroidery hoop, 8". Sewing and tapestry needles. Straight pins. Sewing machine. Steam iron.

MATERIALS

For Each Ornament: Even-weave Aida cloth, 14 squares-to-the-inch, 10"x12" piece white. DMC six-strand embroidery floss, one skein each color in color key. Fine gold metallic thread. Cotton broadcloth, 5"x7" piece white. Satin ribbon ⅛" wide, 17" piece. Sewing thread to match fabric and ribbon. Fiberfill.

DIRECTIONS

To Embroider: To prevent Aida cloth from raveling, bind raw edges with masking tape, whipstitch edges by hand, or zigzag-stitch with sewing machine ⅛" in from edges. With sewing thread, hand-baste two lines on Aida cloth connecting mid-points of pairs of parallel edges to find center of fabric. With short fabric edges at top and bottom, count

38 squares up from center to locate placement of first stitch; mark with straight pin. Place Aida cloth in hoop, centering it, to keep fabric taut.

Work embroidery for each angel following chart and color key and beginning at pin with first cross-stitch in halo, indicated by arrow on chart. Each symbol on chart represents one cross-stitch worked over one square of fabric; different symbols represent different colors of floss, or gold metallic thread. Heavy lines represent backstitches, which are worked after all cross-stitch is complete.

Cut floss and metallic thread into 18" lengths. Separate floss and work cross-stitch with two strands in tapestry needle. Use enough strands metallic thread to equal thickness of two strands floss.

To begin a strand, leave an end on back of fabric and work over it to secure (Fig. 1). When working cross-stitch, work all underneath stitches in one direction and all top stitches in opposite direction (Fig. 2); make sure stitches lie flat and smooth. Work one-quarter and three-quarter cross-stitches where indicated by diagonal lines across symboled squares on chart (Fig. 3).

Let needle hand freely from work now and then to untwist floss or thread.

Fig. 1

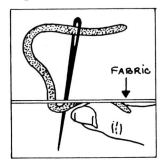

Fig. 2

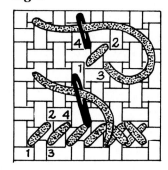

Fig. 3

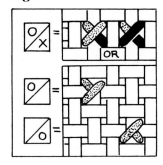

Fig. 4

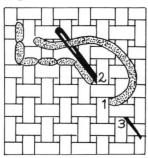

When all cross-stitch is complete, work backstitch (Fig. 4) to outline and define individual design areas. Using same number of strands of metallic thread in needle as before, outline wings with gold. Using one strand of floss, outline hair with medium brown, eyes with dark brown, and top and bottom of hands with medium rose. Stitch gown hem to match gown sides. Work additional backstitching as directed below.

Angel A: Outline sleeves with royal blue. Stitch neck edge and shoulders with forest green.

Angel B: Outline sleeves with medium sea green. Stitch neck edge with medium brown. Stitch collar sides and shoulders with forest green.

Angel C: Outline sleeves and neck edge with medium rose. Stitch shoulders with wine.

When all embroidery is complete, remove fabric from hoop; steam-press gently on wrong side.

To Assemble Ornament: Trace actual-size pattern, marking solid outline only. Glue tracing to cardboard; let dry; cut out, for template. Center template on wrong side of cross-stitch angel; trace and cut out along outline, for ornament front. Cut out matching backing from broadcloth.

Pin ornament front and backing together, wrong sides out, with edges even. Cut 10″ length of ribbon; tie into bow and set aside. Fold remaining 7″ ribbon in half, for hanging loop; adjusting pins as necessary, secure hanging loop between ornament front and backing at center top so that ribbon fold faces ornament bottom and ends are even with ornament top. Referring to original pattern, machine-stitch around sides and top of orna-ment, making ¼″ seam and leaving bottom edge open between dots. Clip into seam allowance along curves; turn piece to right side; hanging loop will extend above ornament. Stuff ornament lightly with fiberfill. Turn raw edges ¼″ to inside; slip-stitch opening closed. Tack bow to ornament top to cover bottom of hanging loop at seam.

Designed by PAM BONO

CROSS-STITCH ANGEL ASSEMBLY

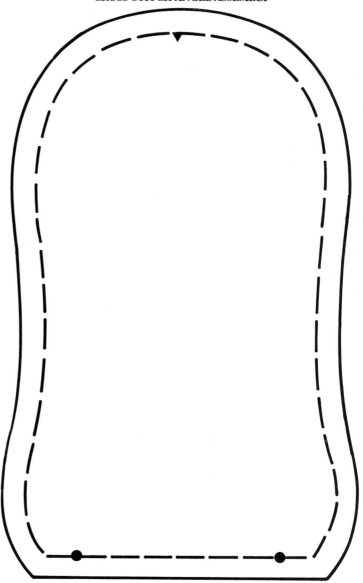

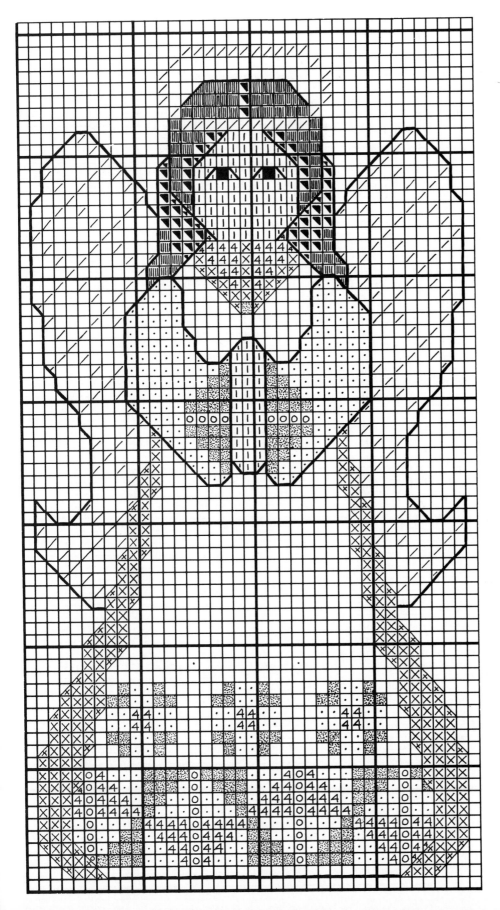

ANGEL A

Color Key

- ⊡ **Pale Orange #754**
- ⊙ **Pale Yellow #677**
- ⋅ **Light Blue #794**
- ▨ **Royal Blue #791**
- ⊠ **Light Sea Green #504**
- ④ **Forest Green #500**
- ⫾⫿ **Light Brown #3032**
- ◣ **Medium Brown #3031**
- ■ **Dark Brown #3371**
- ⊿ **Gold Metallic**

ANGEL B

Color Key

- ⊡ Pale Orange #754
- ③ Medium Rose #223
- ▤ Light Lilac #3042
- ⑧ Dark Lilac #3041
- ⊠ Light Sea Green #504
- ⬚ Medium Sea Green #502
- ④ Forest Green #500
- ⫿⫿⫿ Light Brown #3032
- ◥ Medium Brown #3031
- ■ Dark Brown #3371
- ╱ Gold Metallic

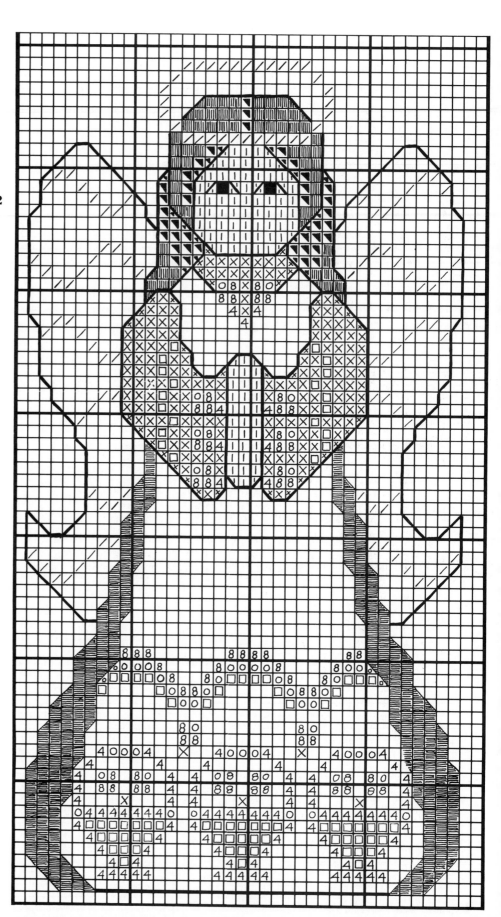

58

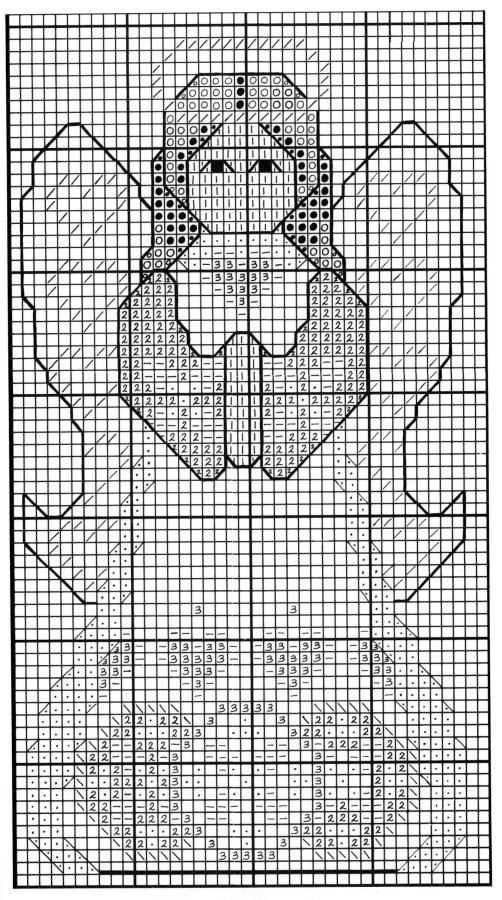

ANGEL C

Color Key

⊡	Pale Orange #754
⊙	Pale Yellow #677
⬤	Honey #680
②	Pale Pink #3713
◧	Light Rose #224
③	Medim Rose #223
⊟	Wine #221
⊡	Light Blue #794
◩	Medium Brown #3031
■	Dark Brown #3371
⊡	Gold Metallic

59

The Christmas Ships

Most people think you can't do much with walnut shells, but when I was a kid my dad used to turn them into sailing ships. Other kids' fathers could do this, too, once they'd seen that all it took was a little melted candle wax in the bottom of a halved shell, a toothpick for the mast, and a square piece of paper for the sail. "Hell, anyone can make these things," my dad would say.

He'd rattle through the walnut bowl looking for the biggest nut, crack it slowly, dig out the meat with those slim silver picks that came with the nutcracker set but which no one else ever used, and he'd hold up the best hull you could imagine: prow pointed, keel deep, stern bridged by the last bit of thin interior shell.

He'd send one of us kids to the hall closet for a spool. "It has to be brown thread. Light brown is better." And he would cut a length of it, push the middle down into the bottom of the shell, and drip wax over it. The wax would cloud and the thread disappear, except for the ends fore and aft, the starts of the rigging. "A frigate," my dad would say, taking scissors and trimming down three toothpicks—the shorter masts and the jib boom—so they wouldn't have ragged ends.

He'd drip more wax in. "Not too much or the thing won't float." When the wax jelled enough, he'd slip in the masts. They would already be fixed with square sails, pushed down to crescents to appear filled with wind. He would cut the spanker and jib sails to the proper shape and glue them to the spars. The wax had to be cold, as hard as a candle again, before he would finish the rigging, tying thread to catch mast top, then quickly snipping off all the loose ends.

This was always around Christmas when there were several large bowls of nuts in the house, and more still in bags in the cupboards. When he was done making three ships, one for each of his boys, my dad would want them painted. Gold, always. We would search our

model paints and bring out the bottles. It took two coats to cover the hulls. Once or twice we spray-painted the ships, sails and all. Then he would hang them on the tree.

"Dad, we want to sail them," I'd say.

"We can make some others to sail," he would tell me.

"Sure, some junk ones."

The ships were beautiful on the tree, floating above the thin glass globes and colored lights. Flying ships like Captain Hook's, dusted gold to lift them into the air.

But ships are meant for sailing, and every boy is a sailor. The golden frigates would end up at the bottom of the tub, each hull weighted down with a marble for a cannonball, masts and sails broken and bobbing on the surface. Five years, maybe, my dad had patience enough to build these ships for us, three to be sunk before Christmas, and three right after.

I have my own son now, and a daughter. Six and five. I tell them tonight about the Christmas ships. We start cracking and sorting the shells. My wife lights a candle. The sails are cut and the box of toothpicks discovered behind the spatulas in the drawer. My son is louder and more enthusiastic. He thinks the first ship is for him. My daughter has been taught that girls are still first. I know that into whichever little hands this homely craft is bound, it is doomed. Both of my children hold the glint of determined foundering in their eyes.

But it doesn't matter. Nothing matters but the building, I realize. I start singing a Christmas song that is not about sailing. I watch the wax drops cloud in the bottom of the shell. For all those ships my dad built for me, I build this one for him.

STEVEN GOLDSBERRY

Doughcraft Ornaments

*Trim the tree with these bright dough ornaments...hang them
on the wall...or tie them to Christmas packages. It's easy and fun
to make the Bouquet...Floral Wreath...Basket...and Christmas Angels.
Thread red and green ribbons through the ornaments —
or use silver and gold ribbons for an elegant look.*

Floral Dough Ornaments
EQUIPMENT

Pencil. Ruler. Compass. Tracing paper, lightweight cardboard, and white glue, for templates. Scissors. Sharp knife. Fine pointed paintbrushes, for paints (optional). Wide, flat brush, for polyurethane.

MATERIALS

Flour/Salt Dough #2 (see recipe). Gold and silver paints (optional). Polyurethane. Ribbon: ⅛″ wide, for threading Braided Strip or Braided Wreath; desired ribbon for hanging loops.

Flour/Salt Dough #2

  1 **pound white flour**
  ½ **pound salt (iodized or plain)**
  1½ **cups water**
      Food coloring, red and green

In big bowl, mix flour and salt until well-blended and smooth. Add 1 cup water and continue to mix. Slowly add remaining water, turning dough in bowl. Push dough into a ball, working in any dry ingredients left in bottom of bowl. Knead dough on floured surface for at least 10 minutes. Divide dough in half; wrap one half tightly in plastic. Divide second half, putting about ¾ of dough into one bowl and remaining ¼ into second bowl. Add green food coloring to larger dough piece; add red to smaller piece; mix colored doughs thoroughly, adding more food coloring as necessary to achieve desired colors. Wrap doughs individually in plastic. (Makes all ornaments shown.)

Ornaments: Prepare templates: Trace actual-size patterns, using ruler to mark straight lines; use compass for circles. Make separate tracings of flower and fir, privet, and holly leaves; mark main outlines of Bouquet, Floral Wreath, and Basket bottom, omitting floral details and "braids" on Basket; mark circles 2¾″ and 4¾″ in diameter for inner and outer Floral Wreath edges; for Bouquet top, use 3½″-diameter circle. Glue tracings to cardboard; let dry; cut out along marked outlines; cut away inside of Floral Wreath.

Make dough. Roll out uncolored dough on lightly floured surface to ³⁄₁₆″ thickness. Cut out Bouquet, Wreath, and Basket bottom: Place lightly floured templates on rolled-out dough; cut out shapes along template edges, using sharp knife. Smooth all cut edges with fingers. Score bottom of Bouquet and Basket, using knife or pencil point. To form "braid" for handle and top and bottom edges of Basket, form dough into long, narrow rope; fold in half and twist rope ends together (see original pattern for sizes). For Braided Strip and Braided Wreath (see color photograph), make larger ropes, twisting and joining at ends as shown; leave enough space to thread ribbon through ropes.

Remove colored dough from plastic; roll out to ³⁄₁₆″ thickness or less. Use templates to cut out red flowers and green leaves as directed below; score as shown. Hand-roll small amounts of red dough to form ½″–⅜″ balls for berries.

Bouquet: Cut out 3 fir leaves, 12–13 privet leaves, 6–7 holly leaves, and 2–3 flowers. Roll 3–5 berries.

Floral Wreath: Cut out 7–8 fir leaves, 12–14 privet leaves, 13–14 holly leaves, and 3 flowers. Roll 11–12 berries.

Basket, Braided Strip, or Braided Wreath: Cut out 3 holly leaves. Roll 3 berries. Join pieces by wetting fingertip with water and moistening shape; press pieces together (see color photograph and patterns for suggested placement). For Bouquet and Floral Wreath, make hole in ornament top for threading hanging loop.

Place assembled ornaments on flour-dusted cookie sheet; finish shaping as desired. Bake at medium heat (325°) for one hour, or until hard. Remove ornaments from oven; allow to cool thoroughly.

Decorate ornaments with gold and silver paints as shown or as desired (optional); let dry. When paint is dry, brush on several coats of polyurethane, sealing ornament front and back; let dry thoroughly after applying each coat.

To finish, thread ⅛″ ribbon through braided ornaments as shown. Make and attach ribbon hanging loops to all ornaments.

DESIGNED BY DIANA MANSOUR

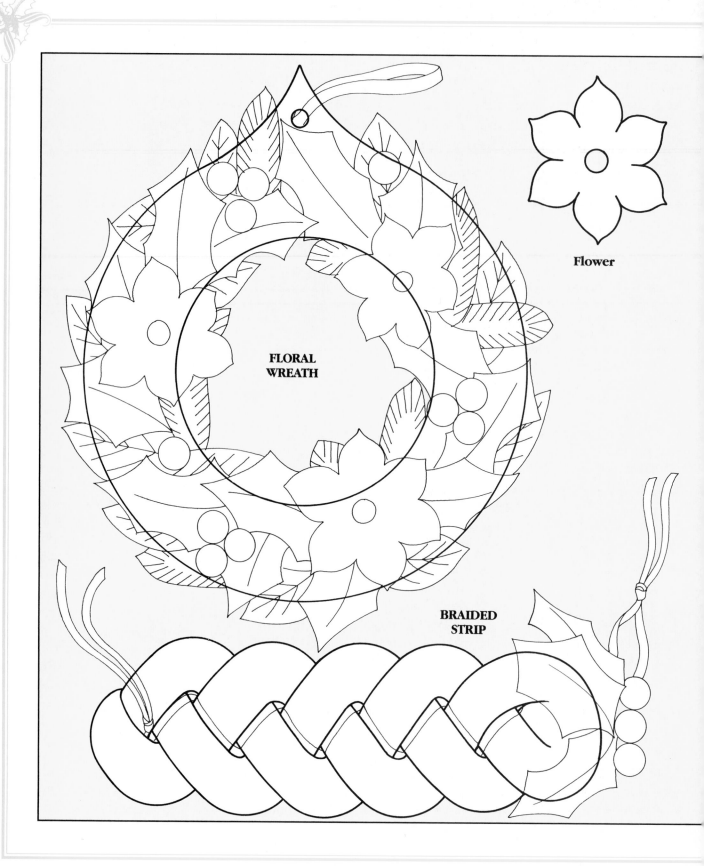

Flower

FLORAL
WREATH

BRAIDED
STRIP

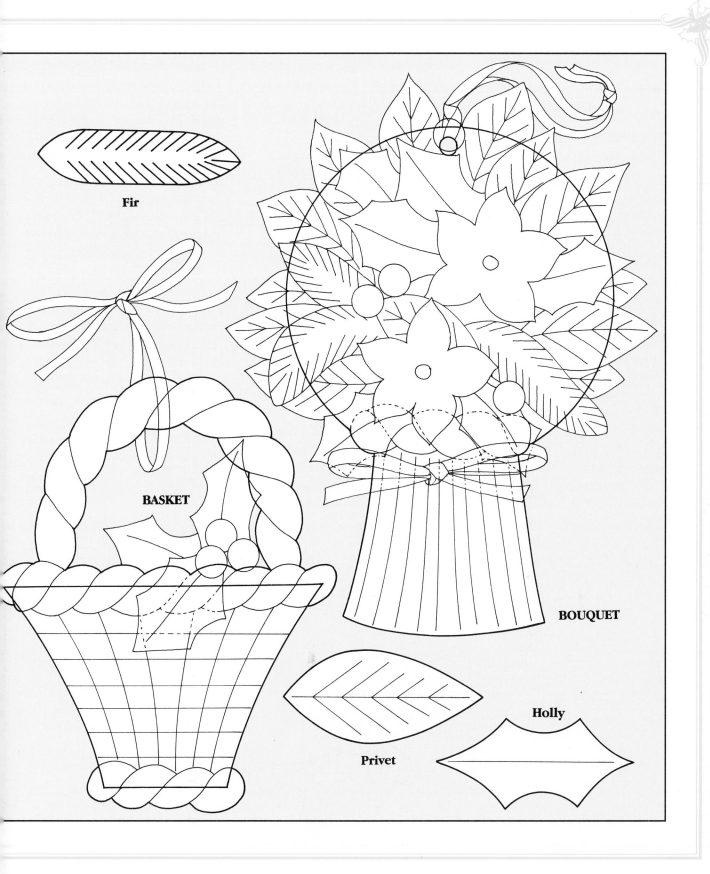

Fir

BASKET

BOUQUET

Privet

Holly

Angel Dough Ornaments

SIZE
Each angel, about 4½"x2½".

EQUIPMENT
Pencil. Tracing paper, lightweight cardboard, and white glue, for templates. Scissors. Sharp knife. Fine pointed paintbrushes, for acrylics. Wide, flat brush, for polyurethane.

MATERIALS
Flour/Salt Dough #1 (see recipe). Acrylic paints. Polyurethane. Fine wire, for hanging loops. Ribbon or cord, for hangers.

Flour/Salt Dough #1
- **3 cups white flour**
- **1 cup salt (iodized or plain)**
- **½ teaspoon powdered alum**
- **1¼ cups water**

In big bowl, mix dry ingredients until well blended and smooth. Add 1 cup water and continue to mix. Slowly add remaining ¼ cup water, turning dough in bowl. Push dough into a ball, working in any dry ingredients left in bottom of bowl. Knead dough on floured surface for at least 10 minutes. Wrap dough tightly in plastic. (Makes 4-6 angels.)

ANGELS
Trace actual-size patterns, making separate tracings for gown, head, hair, wing, sleeve, hand, and horn. Glue tracings to cardboard; let dry. Cut out on outlines, for seven templates.

Make dough. Roll out dough on lightly floured surface to ⅜" thickness. Cut out individual parts for each ornament by placing lightly floured templates on rolled-out dough; cut out shapes along template edges, using sharp knife. Score wing as shown. Smooth and round all cut edges with fingers.

Join shapes to form flying angel with horn, referring to original pattern for placement. To join pieces, wet fingertip with water and use to moisten shapes; press pieces together.

Place assembled angel on flour-dusted cookie sheet; finish shaping as desired. For hanging loop, cut short length wire and form into loop, twisting ends together tightly. Insert wire ends into top edge of hair; see color photograph.

Bake ornaments at medium heat (325°-350°) for about 45 minutes, or until hard. Remove ornaments from oven; allow to cool thoroughly.

Paint angels with acrylic paints as shown or as desired, leaving tan areas in natural cookie color; let dry. When paint is dry, brush on several coats of polyurethane, sealing ornament front and back; let dry thoroughly after applying each coat.

When ornament is thoroughly dry, thread desired length cord or ribbon through hanging loop; tie bow or knot to secure.

Designed by DIANE WAGNER

ANGEL DOUGH ORNAMENT ASSEMBLY

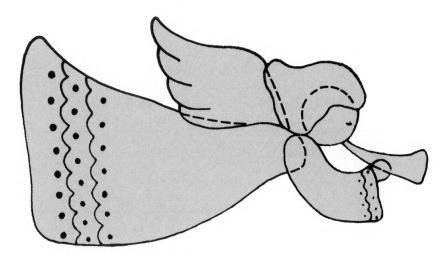

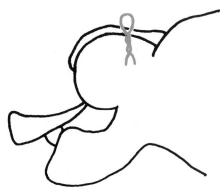

66

Paper Ribbon Angels

· ·

It's great fun making angels by twisting and shaping paper ribbons. For decorations, hang them on a tree or wall...or tape them to gift packages. Or arrange a grouping of angels around an entryway mirror, to welcome all your guests.

SIZE
Angels shown, about 5½″ high.

EQUIPMENT
Ruler. Scissors. Hot glue gun. Toothpicks. Black felt-tip pen (optional).

MATERIALS
For Each 5½″ Angel: Twisted paper ribbon 5″ wide, 22″ length. Wood bead, ⅞″ diameter. Narrow garland, 5½″ length; or metallic ribbon 3⁄16″ wide, 3½″ length. Yellow yarn. Narrow ribbon, cord, or tinsel, 8″ length. Fine wire.

DIRECTIONS
Head and Gown: Cut twisted paper ribbon in half, to form two 11″ lengths. Thread one twisted (unspread) end of a ribbon through bead (head), so that about 4½″ of ribbon (gown front) extends below head with the rest extending above. Spread and untwist ribbon above head; fold over head top and behind gown front, to form hood and gown back. Adjust gown and trim ends as needed to make hem edges even at bottom. Untwist and spread hems to 5″ wide on front and back; leave ribbon gathered at neck edge on gown front. Use hot glue to secure hood to back of head, if desired. (**Note:** If using metallic ribbon, apply hot glue with a toothpick, allowing glue to cool slightly in order to prevent metallic ribbon from being melted by too-hot glue.)

Wings: Untwist and spread entire length of second ribbon. Overlap ribbon ends about ½″, forming a loop; with overlap at center front, pinch center of loop to form bow; wrap center of bow with short length of fine wire, to secure. Insert bow between gown front and back, so that center of bow is at center bottom of head and loops at ends extend equally at gown sides. Glue wings to gown front and back.

Hanging Loop: Fold narrow ribbon, cord, or tinsel in half with ends even. Poke ends into opening on head top for about ¼″, using fingertip or toothpick to wedge hanging loop ends between head and hood front; dot with glue to secure.

Hair: Comb or brush a few short strands of yarn and glue to head front for bangs; trim to desired length.

Halo: Overlap ends of garland or narrow metallic ribbon, to form halo; secure lapped ends and test-fit above angel's head. Adjust size of halo if necessary; glue ends to secure. Place halo on head with ends at center back; apply a dot of glue to hold halo in place on head back.

Face: Use black felt-tip pen to draw eyes, brows, nose, and mouth as shown or as desired, or leave face blank.

Designed by SYDNE MATUS

SPECIAL HINTS

Twisted paper ribbon (which looks like paper rope before being untwisted) is available in crafts stores and comes in various solids, prints, and metallics. It is also available in different widths. The size bead you use for the angel's head should be proportional to the width of the ribbon used for her gown and wings. The garland or narrow metallic ribbon for her halo should be proportional in width to the size of her head.

Noël Stocking

Traditionally beautiful for a child or an adult,
this stocking can be "hung by the chimney with care,
in the hopes that St. Nicholas soon would be there."
The bold and sturdy design will hold plenty
of gaily-wrapped stocking stuffers.

SIZE
Finished stocking, about 11″ high.

EQUIPMENT
Pencil. Ruler. Paper for patterns. Tracing paper. Dressmaker's tracing (carbon) paper. Dry ball-point pen. Scissors. Straight pins. Sewing machine. Steam iron.

MATERIALS
Closely woven cotton fabrics 36″ wide, ⅝ yard each green (for outside of stocking) and white (for lining). Gold tubular cord ⅛″ diameter or less, 1 yard. Sewing thread to match fabrics and cord. Red cotton piping, 1 yard. Batting.

DIRECTIONS
Prepare pattern: Enlarge patterns for stocking top and bottom by copying on paper ruled in 1″ squares; mark outlines, lettered dots, and "Noël," using ruler for straight edges. Make a tracing of enlarged patterns, lining up A-B edges to make one complete stocking pattern.

Cut stocking and lining fabrics in half, to form four rectangles, each ½ yard x ⅝ yard. Transfer tracing of complete stocking to right side of one green rectangle, using dressmaker's carbon and dry ball-point pen; omit fold line; do not cut out until directed.

Use gold sewing thread and cord to couch lines of "Noël" (see Stitch Details), omitting dots over "o"; tack cord ends securely in place. Work French knot dots over "o."

Use tracing to transfer stocking outline and lettered dots to wrong side of second green rectangle. Mark two stockings on wrong side of lining pieces, omitting fold line and reversing tracing for second stocking. Cut out two green and two white stockings on marked outlines; do not add seam allowance. Use one fabric stocking as pattern to cut two same-size stockings from thin layer of batting.

Pin green stocking pieces

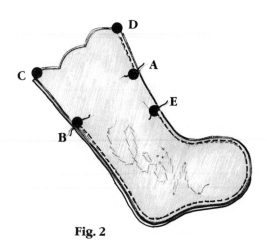

Fig. 2

matching seams and raw top edges. Use zipper foot to machine-stitch B-C-D-C-B edges, working over previous stitching on piping as before.

Pull lining through green stocking to outside, working carefully through front A-E opening; turn green stocking right side out, working through same opening; insert

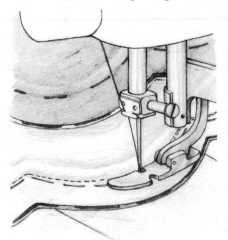

lining into stocking top, matching seams and edges as before. Press raw front edges ⅜" to inside; slipstitch closed with invisible stitches. Fold stocking to outside along A-B line, to form cuff; lightly steampress folded edges.

Make hanging loop: Cut desired length gold ribbon. Fold ribbon in half; tack ends to inside of stocking at B, securing with invisible stitches.

together, wrong sides out, with raw edges even; machine-stitch ⅜" in from edges, leaving A-E and B-C-D-C-B edges open (Fig. 1). Clip into seam allowance; do not turn stocking to right side until directed.

Pin one batting stocking to wrong side of each lining piece; stitch edges together all around with ⅜" seam. Stitch padded lining pieces together, with batting on outside; leave B-C-D-C-B edges open. Trim away excess batting close to stitching, to reduce bulkiness.

Turn lining inside out so that fabric is on the outside. Pin piping to outside of lining on B-C-D-C-B edges, matching raw edges and clipping into seam allowance of piping along curves of fabric for a smooth fit (Fig. 2). Use zipper foot to machine-stitch piping in place, working along stitching line on piping and joining piping edges neatly at B; do not turn stocking to right side until directed.

With green stocking still on wrong side and lining still fabric side out, insert lining into stocking,

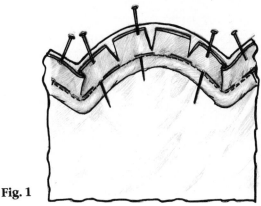

Fig. 1

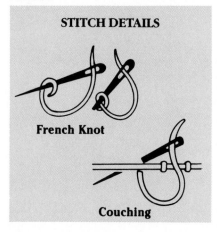

STITCH DETAILS

French Knot

Couching

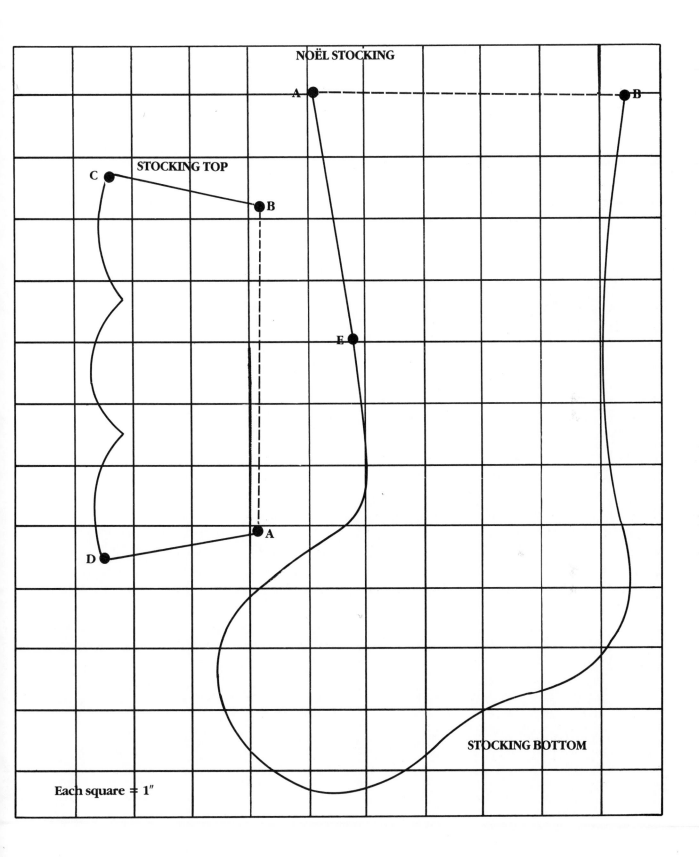

NOËL STOCKING

A •- •B

STOCKING TOP

C •
•B

E •

•A

D •

STOCKING BOTTOM

Each square = 1″

Hold Fast
Your Dreams

On Christmas morn I'd love to reach
Into the clear blue skies,
And fill your stocking up with gifts
To make you great and wise.

But most of all, dear boy, I'd like
To leave this gift with you:
Beware of life's synthetic gains
As years go rushing through.

Remember sunsets over fields,
The fish you caught in streams,
Weed out the glitter, gold is cold...
Hold fast to all your dreams.

ANNETTE VICTORIN

Christmas Every Day

The little girl came into her papa's study, as she always did Saturday morning before breakfast, and asked for a story. He tried to beg off that morning, for he was very busy, but she would not let him. So he began:

"Well, once there was a little pig—"

She put her hand over his mouth and stopped him at the word. She said she had heard little pig-stories till she was perfectly sick of them.

"Well, what kind of story *shall* I tell, then?"

"About Christmas. It's getting to be the season. It's past Thanksgiving already."

"It seems to me," her papa argued, "that I've told as often about Christmas as I have about little pigs."

"No difference! Christmas is more interesting."

"Well!" Her papa roused himself from his writing by a great effort. "Well, then, I'll tell you about the little girl that wanted it Christmas every day in the year. How would you like that?"

"First-rate!" said the little girl; and she nestled into a comfortable shape in his lap, ready for listening.

"Very well, then, this little pig—Oh, what are you pounding me for?"

"Because you said little pig instead of little girl."

"I should like to know what's the difference between a little pig and a little girl that wanted it Christmas every day!"

"Papa," said the little girl, warningly, "if you don't go on, I'll *give* it to you!" And at this her papa darted off like lightning, and began to tell the story as fast as he could.

Well, once there was a little girl who liked Christmas so much that she wanted it to be Christmas every day in the year; and as soon as Thanksgiving was over she began to send postal-cards to the old Christmas Fairy to ask if she mightn't have it. But the old Fairy never answered any of the postals; and after a while the little girl found out that the Fairy was pretty particular, and wouldn't notice anything but letters—not even correspondence cards in envelopes; but real letters on sheets of paper, and sealed outside with a mono-gram—or your initial, anyway. So, then, she began to send her letters; and in about three weeks—or just the day before Christmas, it was—she got a letter from the Fairy, saying she might have it Christmas every day for a year, and then they would see about having it longer.

The little girl was a good deal excited already, preparing for the old-fashioned, once-a-year Christmas that was coming the next day, and perhaps the Fairy's promise didn't make such an impression on her as it would have made at some other time. She just resolved to keep it to herself, and surprise everybody with it as it kept coming true; and then it slipped out of her mind altogether.

She had a splendid Christmas. She went to bed early, so as to let Santa Claus have a chance at the stockings, and in the morning she was up the first of anybody and went and felt them, and found hers all lumpy with packages of candy, and oranges and grapes, and pocket-books and rubber balls, and all kinds of small presents, and her big brother's with nothing but the tongs in them, and her young lady sister's with a new silk umbrella, and her papa's and mamma's with potatoes and pieces of coal wrapped up in tissue-paper, just as they always had every Christmas. Then she waited around till the rest of the family were up, and she was the first to burst into the library, when the doors were opened, and look at the large presents laid out on the library-table—books, and portfolios, and boxes of stationery, and breastpins, and dolls, and little stoves, and dozens of hankerchiefs, and inkstands, and skates, and snow-shovels, and photograph-frames, and little easels, and boxes of water-colors, and Turkish paste, and nougat, and candied cherries, and dolls' houses, and waterproofs—and the big Christmas-tree, lighted and standing in a waste-basket in the middle.

She had a splendid Christmas all day. She ate so much candy that she did not want any breakfast; and the whole forenoon the presents kept pouring in that the expressman had not had time to deliver the night before; and she went round giving the presents she

had got for other people, and came home and ate turkey and cranberry for dinner, and plum-pudding and nuts and raisins and oranges and more candy, and then went out and coasted, and came in with a stomach-ache, crying; and her papa said he would see if his house was turned into that sort of fool's paradise another year; and they had a light supper, and pretty early everybody went to bed cross.

Here the little girl pounded her papa in the back, again.

"Well, what now? Did I say pigs?"

"You made them *act* like pigs."

"Well, didn't they?"

"No matter; you oughtn't to put it into a story."

"Very well, then, I'll take it all out."

Her father went on:

The little girl slept very heavily, and she slept very late, but she was wakened at last by the other children dancing round her bed with their stockings full of presents in their hands.

"What is it?" said the little girl, and she rubbed her eyes and tried to rise up in bed.

"Christmas! Christmas! Christmas!" they all shouted, and waved their stockings.

"Nonsense! It was Christmas yesterday."

Her brothers and sisters just laughed. "We don't know about that. It's Christmas to-day, anyway. You come into the library and see."

Then all at once it flashed on the little girl that the Fairy was keeping her promise, and her year of Christmases was beginning. She was dreadfully sleepy, but she sprang up like a lark—a lark that had overeaten itself and gone to bed cross—and darted into the library. There it was again! Books, and portfolios, and boxes of stationery, and breastpins—

"You needn't go over it all, papa; I guess I can remember just what was there," said the little girl.

Well, and there was the Christmas-tree blazing away, and the family picking out their presents, but looking pretty sleepy, and her father perfectly puzzled, and her mother ready to cry. "I'm sure I don't see how I'm to dispose of all these things," said her mother, and her father said it seemed to him they had had something just like it the day before, but he supposed he must have dreamed it. This struck the little girl as the best kind of a joke; and so she ate so much candy she didn't want any breakfast, and went round carrying presents, and had turkey and cranberry for dinner, and then went out and coasted, and came in with a—

"Papa!"

"Well, what now?"

"What did you promise, you forgetful thing?"

"Oh! oh yes!"

Well, the next day, it was just the same thing over again, but everybody getting crosser; and at the end of a week's time so many people had lost their tempers that you could pick up lost tempers anywhere; they perfectly strewed the ground. Even when people tried to recover their tempers they usually got somebody else's, and it made the most dreadful mix.

The little girl began to get frightened, keeping the secret all to herself; she wanted to tell her mother, but she didn't dare to; and she was ashamed to ask the Fairy to take back her gift, it seemed ungrateful and ill-bred, and she thought she would try to stand it, but she hardly knew how she could, for a whole year. So it went on and on, and it was Christmas on St. Valentine's Day and Washington's Birthday, just the same as any day, and it didn't skip even the First of April, though everything was counterfeit that day, and that was some *little* relief.

After a while coal and potatoes began to be awfully scarce, so many had been wrapped up in tissue-paper to fool papas and mammas with. Turkeys got to be about a thousand dollars apiece—

"Papa!"

"Well, what?"

"You're beginning to fib."

"Well, *two* thousand, then."

And they got to passing off almost anything for turkeys—half-grown humming-birds, and even rocs out of the *Arabian Nights*—the real turkeys were so scarce. And cranberries—well, they asked a diamond apiece for cranberries. All the woods and orchards were cut down for Christmas-trees, and where the woods and orchards used to be it looked just like a stubble-field, with the stumps. After a while they had to make Christmas-trees out of rags, and stuff them with bran, like old-fashioned dolls; but there were plenty of rags, because people got so poor, buying presents for one another, that they couldn't get any new clothes, and they just wore their old ones to tatters. They got so poor that everybody had to go to the poor-house, except the confectioners, and the fancy-store keepers, and the picture-book sellers, and the expressmen; and *they* all got so rich and proud that they would hardly wait upon a person when he came to buy. It was perfectly shameful!

Well, after it had gone on about three or four months, the little girl, whenever she came into the room in the morning and saw those great ugly, lumpy stockings dangling at the fireplace, and the disgusting presents around everywhere, used to just sit down and burst out crying. In six months she was perfectly exhausted; she couldn't even cry any more; she just lay on the lounge and rolled her eyes and panted. About the beginning of October she took to sitting down on dolls wherever she found them—French dolls, or any kind—she hated the sight of them so; and by Thanksgiving she was crazy, and just slammed her presents across the room.

By that time people didn't carry presents around

nicely any more. They flung them over the fence, or through the window, or anything; and, instead of running their tongues out and taking great pains to write "For dear Papa," or "Mamma," or "Brother," or "Sister," or "Susie," or "Sammie," or "Billie," or "Bobbie," or "Jimmie," or "Jennie," or whoever it was, and troubling to get the spelling right, and then signing their names, and "Xmas, 18—," they used to write in the gift-books, "Take it, you horrid old thing!" and then go and bang it against the front door. Nearly everybody had built barns to hold their presents, but pretty soon the barns overflowed, and then they used to let them lie out in the rain, or anywhere. Sometimes the police used to come and tell them to shovel their presents off the sidewalk, or they would arrest them.

"I thought you said everybody had gone to the poor-house," interrupted the little girl.

"They did go, at first," said her papa; "but after a while the poor-houses got so full that they had to send the people back to their own houses. They tried to cry, when they got back, but they couldn't make the least sound."

"Why couldn't they?"

"Because they had lost their voices, saying 'Merry Christmas' so much. Did I tell you how it was on the Fourth of July?"

"No; how was it?" And the little girl nestled closer, in expectation of something uncommon.

Well, the night before, the boys stayed up to celebrate, as they always do, and fell asleep before twelve o'clock, as usual, expecting to be wakened by the bells and cannon. But it was nearly eight o'clock before the first boy in the United States woke up, and then he found out what the trouble was. As soon as he could get his clothes on he ran out of the house and smashed a big cannon-torpedo down on the pavement; but it didn't make any more noise than a damp wad of paper; and after he tried about twenty or thirty more, he began to pick them up and look at them. Every single torpedo was a big raisin! Then he just streaked it upstairs, and examined his firecrackers and toy pistol and two-dollar collection of fireworks, and found that they were nothing but sugar and candy painted up to look like fireworks! Before ten o'clock every boy in the United States found out that his Fourth of July things had turned into Christmas things; and then they just sat

down and cried—they were so mad. There are about twenty million boys in the United States, and so you can imagine what a noise they made. Some men got together before night, with a little powder that hadn't turned into purple sugar yet, and they said they would fire off *one* cannon, anyway. But the cannon burst into a thousand pieces, for it was nothing but rock-candy, and some of the men nearly got killed. The Fourth of July orations all turned into Christmas carols, and when anybody tried to read the Declaration, instead of saying, "When in the course of human events it becomes necessary," he was sure to sing, "God rest you, merry gentlemen." It was perfectly awful.

The little girl drew a deep sigh of satisfaction.

"And how was it at Thanksgiving?"

Her papa hesitated. "Well, I'm almost afraid to tell you. I'm afraid you'll think it's wicked."

"Well, tell, anyway," said the little girl.

Well, before it came Thanksgiving it had leaked out who had caused all these Christmases. The little girl had suffered so much that she had talked about it in her sleep; and after that hardly anybody would play with her. People just perfectly despised her, because if it had not been for her greediness it wouldn't have happened; and now, when it came Thanksgiving, and she wanted them to go to church, and have squash-pie and turkey, and show their gratitude, they said that all the turkeys had been eaten up for her old Christmas dinners, and if she would stop the Christmases, they would see about the gratitude. Wasn't it dreadful? And the very next day the little girl began to send letters to the Christmas Fairy, and then telegrams, to stop it. But it didn't do any good; and then she got to calling at the Fairy's house, but the girl that came to the door always said, "Not at home," or "Engaged," or "At dinner," or something like that; and so it went on till it came to the old once-a-year Christmas Eve. The little girl fell asleep, and when she woke up in the morning—

"She found it was all nothing but a dream," suggested the little girl.

"No, indeed!" said her papa. "It was all every bit true!"

"Well, what *did* she find out, then?"

"Why, that it wasn't Christmas at last, and wasn't ever going to be, any more. Now it's time for breakfast."

The little girl held her papa fast around the neck.

"You sha'n't go if you're going to leave it *so*!"

"How do you want it left?"

"Christmas once a year."

"All right," said her papa; and he went on again.

Well, there was the greatest rejoicing all over the country, and it extended clear up into Canada. The people met together everywhere, and kissed and cried for joy. The city carts went around and gathered up all the candy and raisins and nuts, and dumped them into the river; and it made the fish perfectly sick; and the whole United States, as far out as Alaska, was one blaze of bonfires, where the children were burning up their gift-books and presents of all kinds. They had the greatest *time*!

The little girl went to thank the old Fairy because she had stopped its being Christmas, and she said she hoped she would keep her promise and see that Christmas never, never came again. Then the Fairy frowned, and asked her if she was sure she knew what she meant; and the little girl asked her, Why not? And the old Fairy said that now she was behaving just as greedily as ever, and she'd better look out. This made the little girl think it all over carefully again, and she said she would be willing to have it Christmas about once in a thousand years; and then she said a hundred, and then she said ten, and at last she got down to one. Then the Fairy said that was the good old way that had pleased people ever since Christmas began, and she was agreed. Then the little girl said, "What're your shoes made of?" And the Fairy said, "Leather." And the little girl said, "Bargain's done forever," and skipped off, and hippity-hopped the whole way home, she was so glad.

"How will that do?" asked the papa.

"First-rate!" said the little girl; but she hated to have the story stop, and was rather sober.

However, her mamma put her head in at the door, and asked her papa, "Are you never coming to breakfast? What have you been telling that child?"

"Oh, just a moral tale."

The little girl caught him around the neck again.

"*We* know! Don't you tell *what*, papa! Don't you tell *what*!"

WILLIAM DEAN HOWELLS

"Picture Pretty" Pinafore Bib

. . . .

The sweet child in your life will delight in wearing this pinafore bib. And you'll want to take snapshots galore when she's all dressed up in holiday finery.

SIZE
Fits child, sizes 2, 4, 6.

EQUIPMENT
Pencil. Ruler. Tracing paper. Dressmaker's tracing (carbon) paper. Dry ball-point pen. Scissors. Embroidery and sewing needles. Straight pins. Sewing machine with zigzag attachment. Steam iron.

MATERIALS
Cotton broadcloth, linen, or piqué, 45" wide, ½ yard white, for bib. Closely woven cotton fabrics, 6" square green and 3" square yellow, for appliqués. Sewing threads to match fabrics. White flat cotton eyelet lace, 1¼" wide, 2½ yards; ½" wide, ¾ yard. White entredeux with ½"-wide batiste edges, 3 yards. White lightweight interfacing, 10" square white. White fusible webbing. White satin ribbon ¾" wide, 1¾ yards. Three small round buttons, white or clear. Six-strand cotton or silk embroidery floss, small amounts of desired colors, for balls on tree appliqué.

DIRECTIONS
To Cut Out Bib: Trace actual-size patterns for bib front and back, marking all lines and using ruler for straight edges; mark one back with solid line as center back; mark second back pieces in similar manner, but reversing left and right backs, for facing. Pin bib and facing together, wrong sides out, with edges even. Stitch straight (outer) edges; leave curved neck edge open. Clip into seam allowance at inside corners; clip across outside corners. Turn bib to right side; press. Baste neck edge through both fabric layers.

To Trim Outer Edges: With right sides face up, attach entredeux (Fig. 1) to extend straight bib edges; do not join to neck edge until directed: Work on one bib edge at a time; do not attempt to turn corners with entredeux. For each edge, cut matching length entredeux, allowing one extra hole at each end. Cut away one batiste edge. Butt cut edge of entredeux against bib edge, centering it; set machine for narrow zigzag stitches spaced so that needle enters every hole on entredeux and catches edge of bib as shown; zigzag-stitch edge. Cut away remaining batiste, leaving only the row of holes attached to the fabric edge. Join entredeux to adjacent bib edges in same manner, overlapping extra hole at end of length just stitched; trim away batiste.

When entredeux has been stitched to all straight edges, baste one edge of wide flat lace; gather to fit entredeux all around bib, allowing ½" extra at each end for hems; arrange gathers evenly, then topstitch close to gathered edge; make another line of topstitching just inside first one. Press lace ends to wrong side twice; hemstitch. Working on right side of bib and lace, butt gathered edge of lace against entredeux, beginning and ending at center back neck edges; zigzag-stitch by machine as before (Fig. 2), or whipstitch lace to entredeux by hand.

To Trim Neck Edge: Cut a length of entredeux to fit bib neck. Pin entredeux to neck edge, wrong sides out, matching outer edges of bib fabric and batiste. Reset machine for straight stitches; stitch along outer edge of row of holes on entredeux (Fig. 3). Clip into outer batiste edge (seam allowance) so that entredeux lies flat. Trim seam allowance to ¼". Set machine for zigzag stitches wide enough to enter the line of stitches just made on entredeux, and to

clear the raw neck edge; zigzag-stitch to roll and neatly finish edge. Press entredeux to right side, so that remaining batiste edge extends beyond neckline; press seam allowance toward bib. Reset machine for tiny zigzag stitches. With bib face up, stitch over seamline just made, catching seam allowance underneath with stitches. Cut away remaining batiste edge of entredeux.

Gather narrow flat lace and attach to entredeux in same manner as wide lace was applied to straight bib edges (Fig. 4.); hem lace ends.

To Finish: Make three buttonholes, evenly spaced, on wider half of bib back, close to center back edge. Sew three buttons to corresponding points on narrower bib back.

Cut ribbon into four equal lengths, for ties. Press one with dash line as center back. Fold white bib fabric in half, wrong side out. Use dressmaker's carbon and dry ballpoint pen to transfer both backs and two fronts to doubled fabric,

matching center front on pattern with fold on fabric; place pieces at least 1″ apart. Cut out pieces (two fronts and four backs, for bib and facing), adding ½″ seam allowance.

To Appliqué: Make separate tracings of tree and tree-top star. Fuse interfacing to wrong side of appliqué fabrics, following manufacturer's directions. Transfer patterns to right side of fabrics, marking tree on green and star on yellow; cut out. adding ¼″ seam allowance.

Pin tree appliqué to lower left corner of one bib front on right side of fabric; pin star above tree; see color photograph for placement. Machine-stitch appliqués in place along marked outlines, using matching sewing threads and tiny straight stitches. Trim away excess fabric to ⅛″ or less from straight stitching. Set machine for closely spaced zigzag stitches (¼″ wide or less). Using white or desired color thread, zigzag-stitch around appliqués, covering lines of straight stitching and excess fabric; zigzag-stitch bottom edges of tree branches.

Use 4–6 strands floss in needle to work a French knot for each ball on tree (see stitch details).

To Assemble Bib: Pin a left and a right bib back to appliquéd bib front with wrong sides out, matching shoulder edges. Stitch shoulders, making ½″ seams; press seams open. Join remaining end of each tie ⅛″ to wrong side twice; topstitch. Stitch raw end of a tie to each bottom corner of bib front and back on inside, to hide joining.

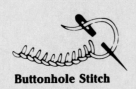

Buttonhole Stitch

French Knot

Outline (Stem) Stitch

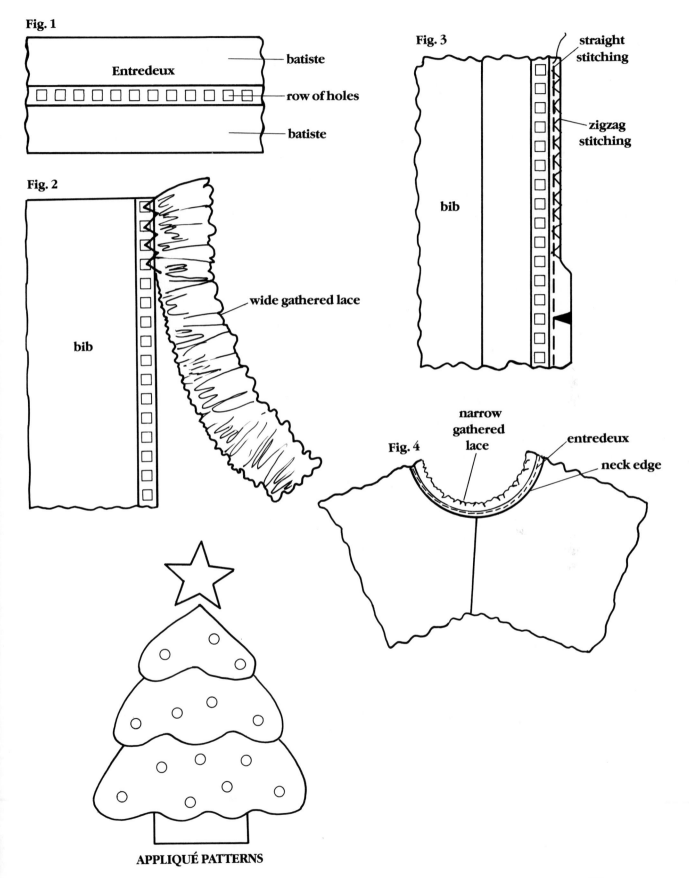

Fig. 1

Entredeux

- batiste
- row of holes
- batiste

Fig. 2

bib

wide gathered lace

Fig. 3

bib

- straight stitching
- zigzag stitching

Fig. 4

narrow gathered lace

- entredeux
- neck edge

APPLIQUÉ PATTERNS

83

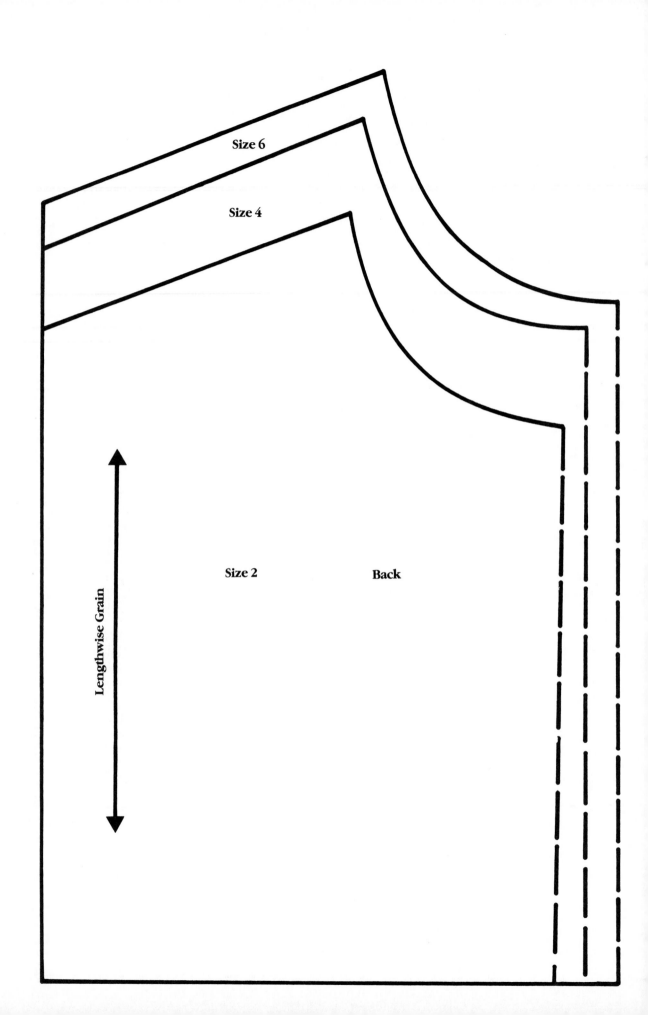

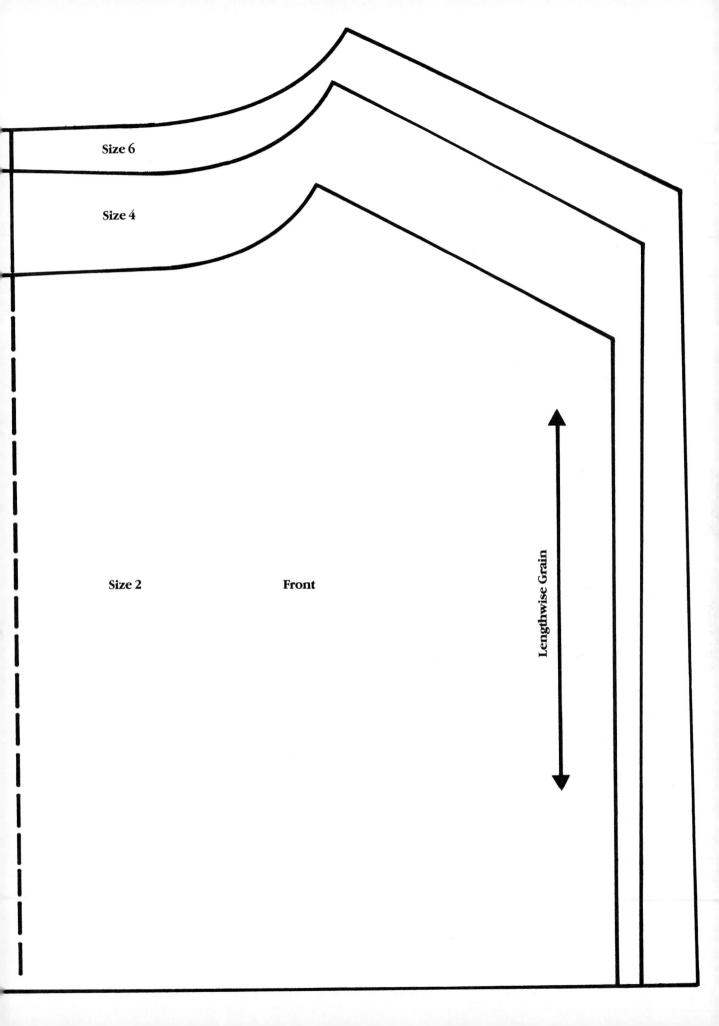

Size 6

Size 4

Size 2

Front

Lengthwise Grain

Susannah Dolly

∙ ∙

*Susannah is a small fabric doll with a winning smile.
Can't you just see her peeking out of a Christmas stocking?
Susannah is wearing a perky bonnet — and she's ready
to spend a lot of time playing let's pretend.*

SIZE
Finished doll, 5″ high.

EQUIPMENT
Pencil. Ruler. Tracing paper. Dressmaker's tracing (carbon) paper. Dry ball-point pen. Scissors. Sewing and embroidery needles. Straight pins. Sewing machine. Iron. Small crochet hook, for turning and stuffing doll.

MATERIALS
Closely woven cotton fabrics: scraps of tiny floral print (for dress and bonnet), dark solid to coordinate with print (for legs), and flesh color (for face and hands). Sewing threads to match fabrics. Satin ribbon ⅛″ wide, ½ yard to coordinate with print, for belt. Six-strand embroidery floss: one skein desired color, for hair; scraps of blue and rose pink, for eyes and mouth. Fiberfill.

DIRECTIONS

To Cut Out Pieces: Trace actual-size patterns, using ruler to mark straight solid, dotted, and dash lines; mark all lines, dots, arrows, and letters. Transfer all patterns to wrong side of fabric, using dressmaker's carbon and dry ballpoint pen; place pieces at least ½″ from fabric edges and ½″ apart: On print fabric, mark one bodice front, one bonnet/bodice back, and two brims; also mark 2½″x9½″ rectangle, for skirt. On dark solid, mark two pairs of legs. On flesh color, mark one face and four hands. Cut out fabric pieces, adding ¼″ at each edge for seam allowance.

To Assemble Doll: Assemble doll as directed below. To join fabric pieces, pin them together, wrong sides out, matching raw edges and markings; baste. Stitch pieces together along marked seamlines by hand or machine, using matching sewing threads and making ¼″ seams unless otherwise directed. Clip into seam allowances at curved edges to ³⁄₁₆″; be very careful not to cut into stitches. Steam- or finger-press seams to one side, toward darker fabric.

Join a hand to each wrist of bodice front and bonnet/bodice back at A-B edges. Join face to bodice front between C's (neck). Join bodice front to one pair of legs along D-E-D edge (waist).

Fold and press bonnet/bodice back in half, wrong side out, along center (dotted) line E-F. Stitch dart from F to G; clip into seam allow-ance at G's. Slit bodice back between E and G. Above G's, press dart to one side; below G's, fold and press edges ¼″ to wrong side.

Stitch brims together around H-H; (outer) edge; turn to right side; press flat. Topstitch brim close to fold; baste through both layers at H-J-H (inner) edge. On bonnet, baste a line of stitching around H-J-H edge; pull stitches, gathering edge to match H-J-H on brim; join.

Join bodice back to second pair of legs along D-E-D edge. Turn doll to right side, working through opening at center back and using crochet hook to help push through hands and feet. Also use hook to push a tiny bit of fiberfill into each hand, stuffing very loosely; top-stitch wrists along seamlines. Stuff remainder of doll firmly. Slip-stitch opening closed, making tiny invisible stitches.

Facial Features: Use one or two strands floss in needle to fill eyes solidly in satin stitch. Use one strand and tiny straight stitches, backstitches, or outline stitch to work mouth.

Hair: Cut six 8″ lengths of unseparated six-strand floss; bundle together with ends even. Using several strands of matching floss in

SUSANNAH DOLL

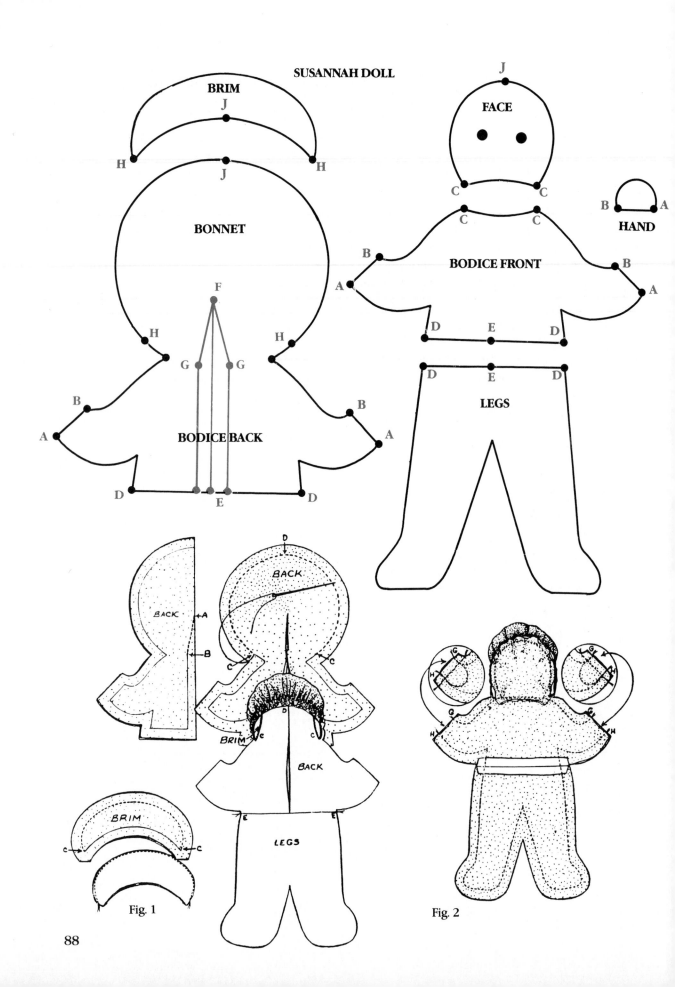

BRIM

J

H   H

BONNET

J

F

FACE

J

C   C

C   C

BODICE FRONT

B   B

A   A

D   E   D

HAND

B   A

H   H

G   G

B   B

A   A

BODICE BACK

D   D

E

D   E   D

LEGS

BACK ←A

BACK

←B

D

C   C

BRIM   C   C

BACK

BRIM

C ←   → C

LEGS

E   E

G   G

H   H

H   H

Fig. 1

Fig. 2

88

needle, tack center of bundle to center of forehead, close to brim seam. Tack "hair" to each side of face, at bottom of brim; see color photograph. Divide hair on each side of face into three equal sections; braid, then secure ends with floss. For bangs, make 3-5 turkey work loops across forehead; cut loops, brush, then trim bangs to desired length.

To Finish: Cut 12″ length ribbon; place around doll's waist for sash; tie bow at center back. Tack a short length of ribbon around bonnet top, if desired, to cover bonnet/brim joining. Tie a few strands of floss around doll's neck, if desired, or tie a small floss bow and tack to neck at center front.

Designed by COLETTE WOLFF

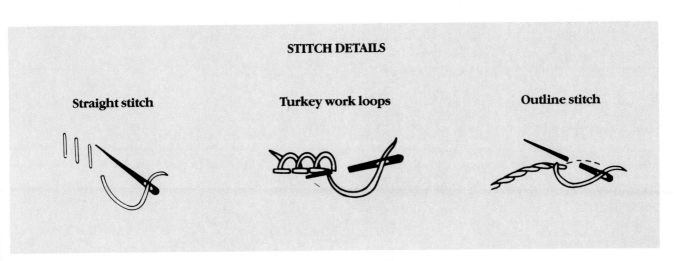

STITCH DETAILS

Straight stitch **Turkey work loops** **Outline stitch**

Snowy Day Helmet

Warm and colorful, this knitted child's hat is perfect for wintry weather. Textured yarn and vibrant color combinations make this helmet a very special Christmas gift.

SIZE

Fits child, ages 2-4.

EQUIPMENT

Circular needle No. 7 (4.5 mm). Four dp needles. Aluminum crochet hook size 5/F. Tapestry needle.

MATERIALS

Knitted worsted weight yarn: 4 oz. main color; 2 oz. each of 8 colors, at least one of which should be bouclé, hand-spun, or other textured yarn. We used wine (MC), yellow loop yarn (A), purple (B), dark aquamarine (C), plum (D), forest green bouclé (E), black (F), light blue (G), and turquoise (H).

GAUGE

9 st sts = 2"; 13 rows = 2". 4 sc = 1"; 5 rows = 1".

HELMET

With MC and circular needle, cast on 80 sts. Work helmet in stockinette st (k each rnd). Cut and join yarns as needed.

Rnds 1–3: With MC, k 3 rnds.

Rnd 4: With A, k around.

Rnds 5 and 6: With B, k around. Do not cut B; join C.

Rnd 7: *With B, k 1; with C, k 1; repeat from * around.

Rnd 8: With B, k around.

Rnd 9: With A, k around.

Rnds 10 and 11: With D, k 2 rnds.

Rnd 12: With E, k around

Rnd 13: With MC, k around. Do not cut MC; join F.

Rnd 14: *With F, k 1; with MC, k 1; repeat from * around.

Rnd 15: With MC, k around.

Rnd 16: With A, k around.

Rnd 17 and 18: With G, k 2 rnds. Do not cut G; join H.

Rnd 19: *With G, k 1; with H, k 1; repeat from * around.

Rnd 20: With G, k around.

Rnd 21: With F, k around.

Rnd 22: With C, k around.

Rnd 23: With MC, k around. Do not cut MC; join A.

Rnd 24: *With A, k 1; with MC, k 1; repeat from * around.

Rnd 25: With MC, k around.

Rnd 26: With E, k around.

Rnd 27: With B, k around.

Rnd 28: * K 3, k 2 tog (dec); repeat from * around — 64 sts.

Rnd 29: With A, k around.

Rnd 30: With B, k around.

Rnd 31: *With H, k 2, k 2 tog; repeat from * around — 48 sts. Do not cut H; join F.

Rnd 32: Divide sts evenly on 4 dp needles. * With H, k 1; with F, k 1; repeat from * around.

Rnd 33: With H, k around.

Rnd 34: * With MC, k 2; k 2 tog; repeat from * around — 32 sts.

Rnd 35: K around.

Rnd 36: With D, k around.

Rnd 37: * K 2 tog; repeat from * around — 16 sts.

Rnd 38: With E, k around.

Rnd 39: With G, k around.

Rnd 40: * K 2 tog; repeat from * around — 8 sts.

Rnd 41: K around.

Rnd 42: With A, k around.

Rnds 43–45: With B, k 3 rnds. Cut yarn; draw end through remaining sts, gather sts tog tightly, and secure end.

Helmet Bottom: Count and mark off 24 sts to left and right of first/last cast-on sts. With MC and crochet hook, sc in each cast-on st between markers — 48 sts. Ch 1, turn. Work even in sc for 13 more rows. Beginning at one end of last sc row with A, sc in each st around all edges.

Ties (make 2): Cut 6 30" lengths of MC. Using tapestry needle, thread strands through one bottom corner of helmet; even yarn ends; tie knot to anchor to corner. Divide yarn into 3 equal sections; braid to within 1½" from ends; knot to secure.

Tassel: Cut one 8" length each of MC, B, and H. Thread strands through point at helmet top; even ends; knot to anchor. Divide strands into 3 sections of one color each; braid; knot end.

Designed by KAREN BUCKHOLZ

Sewing Circle Bag

· ·

*A "carry-along" bag for small sewing supplies…or use soft and
pale fabrics to make a jewelry case. It's the perfect handmade gift
for a woman who loves beautiful things.*

SIZE

Bag, about 4¾" diameter.

EQUIPMENT

Pencil. Ruler. Compass. Lightweight cardboard. Tailor's chalk. Scissors. Straight pins. Sewing needles. Sewing machine. Iron. Tiny safety pin.

MATERIALS

Fabrics 36" wide, ½ yard each print (bag) and coordinating solid (lining). Sewing thread to match fabrics. Satin ribbon ¼" wide, 1½ yards coordinating color. Round plastic lid, such as from coffee can or margarine tub, at least 4½" diameter.

DIRECTIONS

Use compass to mark two circles on cardboard, with diameters of 14" (A) and 11½" (B). Cut along outlines, for two templates. Mark a 4½"-diameter circle (C) on plastic lid; cut out. Use cardboard templates and tailor's chalk to mark one A and one B on each fabric piece; cut out; do not add seam allowance.

Pin fabric A's (one print and one solid) together, wrong sides out, with edges even; stitch ¼" from edges all around, leaving a small opening for turning; clip into seam allowance; turn to right side. Fold raw fabric edges ¼" to inside and slip-stitch opening closed; press. Topstitch ⅛" from edge. Join B's in same manner.

For Ribbon Casing: Form casing on A by making two rows of topstitching, ¾" and 1¼" in from edge (Fig. 1). Fold A in half, print side out, and press to gently crease center line; unfold. For threading holes, make a ½" slit at each end of crease, cutting into print fabric between rows of casing stitches and being careful not to cut into solid fabric or stitching; press out crease.

For Bag Bottom: Use plastic C to mark a circle, centered, on solid fabric side of A. On B, mark 8 "spokes," to divide circle in eighths (Fig. 2). Fold and gently press B in half in both directions to crease; unfold; rotate piece 45° and fold two more times, matching original folds to subdivide quarters and mark eighths; press and unfold. Use ruler and tailor's chalk to mark spokes along fold lines on solid fabric side; press out creases. Place compass point at center of spokes to mark circle, centered on B, with 4¾" diameter. Erase spokes inside circle just drawn.

Stack pieces on work surface with marked (solid fabric) sides of A and B face up: Place A on bottom. Place plastic C on top, following marked circle on fabric for placement. Put B on top, centering it. Use zipper foot to topstitch around marked circle on B, working through fabric layers only and encasing C.

For Pockets: Topstitch spokes from stitching line just made to outer edges of B, working through both fabric layers to form eight pockets.

To Finish: Cut ribbon in half, for two 27" lengths. Attach tiny safety pin to end of one ribbon; use to thread ribbon through casing, entering at one hole and working all around casing and out again at starting hole; remove pin and knot ribbon ends together. Thread remaining ribbon through casing, entering and exiting through opposite hole; remove pin; knot ends (Fig. 3).

To close bag, pull one ribbon with each hand at the same time, grasping knots; top of bag should gather up and close tightly as you pull.

Designed by CHERI TAMM RAYMOND

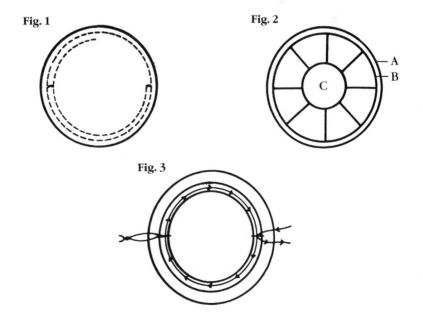

Fig. 1

Fig. 2

Fig. 3

"Antique" Trinket Box

*It's easy to transform a plain, ordinary wooden box
into a charming gift for a friend. A handmade gift is
always appreciated — and the trinket box makes an elegant
and handy catch-all for jewelry or cosmetics.*

SIZE

Box, 6⅜″x4⅞″x3″.

EQUIPMENT

Scissors. Utility knife. Wide, flat brushes for oil paints and wood primer. Stencil brush with soft bristles. Mixing sticks, such as from ice cream pops, or thin dowels. Several small glass jars, such as from baby food. Mineral spirits. Clean, soft rags. Scrap paper. Shallow pan, at least 10″x8″x2″. Spray mounting adhesive. Wood glue. Wood filler. Fine grade sandpaper. Tack cloth.

MATERIALS

Unfinished wood box, 6⅜″x4⅞″x 3″, with hinges and clasp, or box and separately purchased hardware. Precut double mat, 6⅜″x4⅞″, with centered oval openings about 5″x3″ (outer mat) and 4½″x2½″ (inner mat). Wood dollhouse molding, ⅜″x54″. Floral design, such as from greeting card or wallpaper, to fit inner mat opening. Wood primer. Oil paint: dark green, black, burnt umber, and gold metallic. Oil crayon, yellow ocher. Matte varnish.

DIRECTIONS

Remove hardware, if any, from box. Apply two coats wood primer to outside of box and lid, allowing primer to dry and sanding as needed after each coat. Separate the inner and outer oval mats. Paint outside of box, lid, and outer mat with two coats dark green; paint inner mat with two coats gold metallic; let paint dry thoroughly. Attach hinges to box back; attach clasp to box front.

Mottling: Place small amounts dark green and black paints into individual glass jars. Use mineral spirits to thin paints to the consistency of cream.

Fill pan with water to about 1″ deep. Drip thinned paints onto surface of water, working with one color at a time and using clean mixing stick for each color: Dip stick into paint; hold coated stick over water, allowing paint to drip here and there onto surface; some paint may sink to bottom of pan and will not be used in mottling. Use another mixing stick to very gently stir floating colors; paints should spread out and mingle; do not blend together into one solid color.

To transfer paint to box bottom, lower box into pan until bottom just touches surface of water/paint; lift box from pan. Rotate box to mottle sides and lid as for bottom; check water frequently and add more paint as needed. Mottle dark green outer mat in same manner. Touch up any fingerprints on mottled surfaces by blending or blotting with clean rag moistened with mineral spirits. Allow mottling to dry thoroughly.

Lid: Cut out floral design from card or wallpaper, making sure it is large enough so that mats will cover cut edges of design; see color photograph. Spray back of design with mounting adhesive; position design face up and centered on lid top; press in place. Adhere inner mat first and then outer mat to lid in same manner with design centered in mat openings and all outer edges even.

Molding: Place about three tablespoons dark green paint and two or three drops black into a small jar; mix well. Apply two coats of paint mixture to strips; let dry between coats. Add highlights to molding, using gold metallic paint: Dip one corner of rag into paint, then rub into molding, to get paint deep into crevices. Wipe away as much surface paint as desired, using clean section of rag.

Cut molding into eight mitered strips to fit around box bottom and

lid top (see photograph): To cut a strip, hold molding against box and mark box ends on molding. Cut strips on a 45° angle, using utility knife. Referring to photograph, glue molding strips in place on box and lid with wood glue, making sure wood edges are even; let dry, following manufacturer's directions. Fill in any gaps between strips and box, or between strip ends at corners, using wood filler; allow to dry. Sand filler lightly to make smooth; dust with tack cloth. For any areas just sanded that need touching up, apply small amount of paint to clean rag and dab onto box or molding where needed.

Antiquing: Spray all outer sur- faces of box and lid with two light coats matte varnish; let dry after each coat. Sand floral design on box lid very lightly, roughening surface to accept antiquing.

Place small amount burnt umber paint into jar. Dip stencil brush into paint; tap bristles on clean rag or scrap paper until almost dry. Brush paint onto all outer surfaces of box, including floral design, using a cir- cular motion to work color deep into existing paint on box; work from outer edges of box inward, to produce shading.

After antiquing coat is dry, lightly apply yellow ocher crayon to edges of floral design where it meets inner mat, using a circular motion, to give aged appearance to paper.

To finish, apply two more coats matte varnish to box, adding depth and sealing surfaces.

Designed by HOPE EASTMAN

SPECIAL HINTS

Any unfinished wood box, regardless of size or shape, and with or without hardware, can be transformed into an "antique" by using mats, floral designs, and dollhouse molding to fit your particular box.

Directions are given here for antiquing the outside of the box. The inside of the box may be left plain or finished as desired.

Christmas

With Joyful Celebration

Undelivered Gifts

Have you ever had the experience of *almost not doing* an act of thoughtfulness or charity—only to discover later that without this action on your part a very important experience would not have happened to someone else?

Whenever I am tempted to be lazy or indifferent in this way, I inevitably think back to that Christmas in Korea, in 1951.

It was late afternoon on December 24. After a cold, miserable ride by truck in the snow, I was back at our Command Post. Shedding wet clothing, I relaxed on a cot and dozed off. A young soldier came in and in my sleep-fogged condition I heard him say to the clerk, "I wish I could talk to the Sergeant about this."

"Go ahead," I mumbled, "I'm not asleep."

The soldier then told me about a group of Korean civilians four miles to the north who had been forced to leave their burning village. The group included one woman ready to give birth. His information had come from a Korean boy who said these people badly needed help.

My first inner reaction was: How could we ever find the refugees in this snow? Besides, I was dead tired. Yet something told me we should try.

"Go get Crall, Pringle and Graff," I said to the clerk. When these soldiers arrived I told them my plan, and they agreed to accompany me. We gathered together some food and blankets. Then I saw the box of Christmas packages in the corner of the office. They were presents sent over from charity organizations in the States. We collected an armful of packages and started out by jeep.

After driving several miles, the snow became so blinding that we decided to approach the village by foot. After what seemed like hours, we came to an abandoned Mission.

The roof was gone, but the walls were intact. We built a fire in the fireplace, wondering what to do next. Graff opened one of the Christmas packages in which he found some small, artificial Christmas trees and candles. These he placed on the mantel of the fireplace.

I knew it made no sense to go on in this blizzard. We finally decided to leave the food, blankets and presents there in the Mission in the hope that some needy people would find them. Then we groped our way back to the Command Post.

In April 1952, I was wounded in action and taken to the hospital at Won Ju. One afternoon, while basking in the sun, a Korean boy joined me. He was a talkative lad and I only half listened as he rambled on.

Then he began to tell me a story that literally made me jump from my chair. After he finished, I took the boy to our chaplain; he helped me find an elder of the local Korean church who verified the boy's story.

"Yes, it was a true miracle—an act of God," the Korean churchman said. Then he told how on the previous Christmas Eve he was one of a group of Korean civilians who had been wandering about the countryside for days after North Korean soldiers had burned their village. They were nearly starved when they arrived at an old Mission. A pregnant woman in their group was in desperate condition.

"As we approached the Mission, we saw smoke coming from the chimney," the Korean said. "We feared that North Korean soldiers were there, but decided to go in anyway. To our relief, the Mission was empty. But, lo and behold, there were candles on the mantel, along with little trees! There were blankets and boxes of food and presents! It was a miracle!"

The old man's eyes filled with tears as he described how they all got down on their knees and thanked God for their deliverance. They made a bed for the pregnant woman and built a little shelter over her. There

was plenty of wood to burn and food to eat and they were comfortable for the first time in weeks. It was Christmas Eve.

"The baby was born on Christmas Day," the man said. He paused. "The situation couldn't have been too different from that other Birth years ago."

On the following morning American soldiers rescued the Koreans, who later became the nucleus of a Christian church in the village where I was recuperating.

You just never know when you have a special role to play in one of God's miracles.

WAYNE MONTGOMERY

Gifts From
A Christmas Kitchen

· ·

*A gift of food is a gift of love. It shows a thoughtfulness
that no store-bought present can. Use your imagination
to package the gifts...and include the recipe, if you like.*

Chocolate-Raspberry Mini Cakes

- ½ cup seedless red raspberry preserves
- ¼ cup butter *or* margarine, softened
- ½ cup granulated sugar
- 2 eggs
- 1 teaspoon vanilla extract
- 1 cup all-purpose flour
- ⅓ cup unsweetened cocoa
- ¾ teaspoon baking soda
- ½ teaspoon baking powder
- ⅛ teaspoon salt
- ½ cup buttermilk *or* sour milk (Use 1½ teaspoons white vinegar plus milk to equal ½ cup.)
- Vanilla Glaze (follows)

Heat oven to 350°. Lightly spray four 5¾x3¼-inch aluminum foil loaf pans with non-stick cooking spray. In small saucepan, melt preserves over low heat, stirring constantly; set aside. In large mixer bowl, beat butter and sugar until blended. Add eggs and vanilla; beat well. In small bowl, combine flour, cocoa, baking soda, baking powder, and salt; add to butter mixture alternately with buttermilk. Beat 2 minutes. Add preserves; beat until well blended. Pour batter evenly into prepared pans. Bake 25 minutes, or until wooden pick inserted in center comes out clean. Cool completely in pans on wire rack. Make Vanilla Glaze and drizzle in a random pattern over top.

Makes 4 cakes.

Vanilla Glaze

- 1 tablespoon butter *or* margarine
- 1 cup confectioners' sugar
- 1 to 2 tablespoons *hot* water
- ¼ teaspoon vanilla extract

In small saucepan, melt butter over low heat. Add confectioners' sugar alternately with water and vanilla, beating with wire whisk until smooth.

Chocolate Caramels

- ⅔ cup butter *or* margarine
- ½ cup unsweetened cocoa
- 2 cups granulated sugar
- 1 cup light brown sugar (packed)
- 1 cup light cream
- 1 cup light corn syrup
- Coarsely chopped nuts (optional)

Line 9-inch square baking pan with aluminum foil; lightly butter foil. In heavy 3-quart saucepan, melt butter over low heat. Add cocoa; stir until smooth. Remove from heat. Add sugars, cream, and corn syrup; stir until well blended. Cook over medium heat, stirring constantly, until sugars are dissolved. Continue to cook over medium heat, stirring occasionally, to firm-ball stage, 250° on a candy thermometer (or until syrup, when dropped into very cold water, forms a firm ball that does not flatten when removed from water). *Bulb of candy thermometer should not rest on bottom of saucepan.* Pour mixture into prepared pan. Spread nuts evenly over top, if desired, pressing down very lightly. Cool thoroughly. Remove from pan to wooden board; peel off foil. Cut into approximately 1-inch squares with a wet, sharp knife. Wrap individually in plastic wrap.

Makes about 5 dozen caramels.

Favorite Bittersweet Chocolate Sauce

- 1 cup butter *or* margarine
- 1½ cups granulated sugar
- 1¼ cups unsweetened cocoa
- 1 cup heavy cream
- 2 teaspoons vanilla extract

In medium microwave-safe bowl, place butter. Microwave at HIGH (100% power) 1½ minutes, or until melted. Add sugar and cocoa; stir until well blended. Stir in cream. Microwave at HIGH 3 to 4 minutes, stirring after each minute, until sugar is dissolved and mixture is smooth. Stir in vanilla. Serve warm, or cover and refrigerate up to 2 weeks. (Sauce will harden when chilled.)

To reheat, place sauce in microwave-safe bowl. Microwave at HIGH a few seconds at a time until warm. (Time will depend on amount and temperature of sauce.)

Makes about 3 cups sauce.

Chocolate Almond Biscotti

½ cup butter *or* margarine, softened
1¼ cups granulated sugar
2 eggs
1 teaspoon almond extract
2¼ cups all-purpose flour
¼ cup unsweetened cocoa
1 teaspoon baking powder
¼ teaspoon salt
1 cup sliced almonds
Chocolate Glaze (follows)
Vanilla Glaze (follows)
Additional sliced almonds

Heat oven to 350°. In large mixer bowl, beat butter and sugar until well blended. Add eggs and almond extract; beat until smooth. In separate bowl, mix flour, cocoa, baking powder, and salt; blend into butter mixture, beating until smooth. *(Dough will be thick.)* Using wooden spoon, work almonds into dough. Divide dough into two equal halves. With lightly floured hands, shape each half into rectangular log about 2 inches in diameter and 11 inches long. Place on ungreased cookie sheet, at least 2 inches apart. Place on middle oven rack; bake 30 minutes, or until logs are set.

Remove from oven; let cool on cookie sheet 15 minutes. Using serrated knife and a sawing motion, cut logs into ½-inch diagonal slices. Discard end pieces. Reposition oven racks so that they are in the top and middle positions. Arrange slices, cut sides down, close together on two cookie sheets. Place one cookie sheet on each oven rack; bake 8 to 9 minutes. Turn each slice over; switch the position of cookie sheets and continue baking an additional 8 to 9 minutes.

Remove from oven; cool on cookie sheets. Make Chocolate Glaze and dip ends of biscotti in glaze or drizzle glaze over entire cookie. Make Vanilla Glaze and drizzle over chocolate. Garnish with additional almonds, if desired.

Makes 2½ dozen cookies.

Chocolate Glaze

1 package (6 ounces) semi-sweet chocolate pieces
1 tablespoon vegetable shortening

In small microwave-safe bowl, place chocolate pieces and shortening; microwave on HIGH (100% power) 1 to 1½ minutes, or until smooth when stirred.

Makes about 1 cup glaze.

Vanilla Glaze

¼ cup vanilla milk flavored chips
1 teaspoon vegetable shortening

In small microwave-safe bowl, place vanilla chips and shortening; microwave on HIGH (100% power) 30 to 45 seconds, or until smooth when stirred.

Makes about ¼ cup glaze.

Holiday Chocolate Shortbread Cookies

1 cup butter *or* margarine, softened
1¼ cups confectioners' sugar
1 teaspoon vanilla extract
½ cup unsweetened cocoa
1¾ cups all-purpose flour
1 package (10 ounces) vanilla milk flavored chips

Heat oven to 300°. In large mixer bowl, beat butter, sugar, and vanilla until creamy. Add cocoa; blend well. Gradually add flour, stirring until smooth. On lightly floured board, or between two pieces of waxed paper, roll or pat dough to ¼-inch thickness. Using 2-inch cookie cutters, cut in holiday shapes. Reroll dough scraps, cutting cookies until dough is used. Place like shapes and sizes on ungreased cookie sheet. Bake 15 minutes, or just until firm. Immediately place vanilla chips, flat side down, in decorative design on warm cookies. Cool slightly; remove from cookie sheet to wire rack. Cool completely. Store in airtight container.

Makes 4½ dozen cookies.

Triple Decker Fudge

1 package (10 ounces) milk chocolate chunks
1 package (10 ounces) semisweet chocolate chunks
1 package (10 ounces) vanilla milk flavored chips
2 cans (14 ounces each) sweetened condensed milk (not evaporated)

Line 13 x 9-inch pan with aluminum foil. Into three separate medium microwave-safe bowls, place milk chocolate chunks, semisweet chocolate chunks and vanilla milk chips. Into both bowls containing chocolate chunks, pour ¾ cup sweetened condensed milk; into bowl containing vanilla chips, pour remaining sweetened condensed milk. Microwave milk chocolate chunks mixture at HIGH (100% power) 1 minute; stir vigorously. If chunks are not melted, microwave at HIGH additional 15 seconds, or until mixture is smooth when stirred; spread evenly in prepared pan. Repeat microwave procedure with vanilla chips mixture; spread carefully over previous layer. Repeat procedure with semi-sweet chunks layer. Cover; refrigerate until firm. Remove from pan; peel off foil. Cut into 1-inch squares. Store in refrigerator.

Makes about 8 dozen squares.

CONVENTIONAL DIRECTIONS

Prepare pan as directed above. Into three separate medium bowls, place chunks and chips as directed above. In top of double boiler, over hot (not boiling) water, heat sweetened condensed milk until hot; *do not boil*. Into milk chocolate chunks bowl, pour ¾ cup hot sweetened condensed milk; beat mixture until chunks are melted. Spread in prepared pan. Into vanilla chips bowl, pour 1 cup hot sweetened condensed milk; beat mixture until chips are melted. Carefully pour over milk chocolate layer. Into semisweet chocolate chunks bowl, pour remaining hot sweetened condensed milk. Carefully pour over vanilla layer. Refrigerate and store as directed above.

Chocolate Chip Candy Cookie Bars

    1⅔ cups all-purpose flour
      2 tablespoons plus 1½ cups
            granulated sugar
     ¾ teaspoon baking powder
      1 cup cold butter *or* margarine
      1 egg, slightly beaten
      2 tablespoons plus ½ cup
            (5-ounce can) evaporated
            milk (not condensed)
      2 packages (12 ounces each)
            semisweet chocolate pieces
     ½ cup light corn syrup
    1½ cups sliced almonds

Heat oven to 375°. In medium bowl, mix flour, 2 tablespoons sugar, and baking powder; cut in ½ cup butter with pastry blender until mixture forms coarse crumbs. Stir in egg and 2 tablespoons evaporated milk; stir until mixture holds together in ball shape. Press onto bottom and ¼-inch up sides of 15x10-inch jelly roll pan. Bake 8 to 10 minutes, or until lightly browned; remove from oven, leaving oven on. Sprinkle 1½ cups chocolate pieces evenly over crust; *do not press chocolate*; set aside. In 3-quart saucepan, place remaining 1½ cups sugar, remaining ½ cup butter, remaining ½ cup evaporated milk, and corn syrup.

Cook over medium heat, stirring constantly, until mixture boils; stir in almonds. Continue cooking and stirring to 240° on candy thermometer (soft-ball stage), or until mixture, when dropped into very cold water, forms soft ball that flattens when removed from water. Remove from heat. Immediately spoon almond mixture evenly over chocolate and crust; *do not spread*.

Bake 10 to 15 minutes, or just until almond mixture is golden brown. Remove from oven; cool 5 minutes. Sprinkle with remaining ½ cup chocolate pieces; cool completely. Cut into approximately 1x4-inch bars.

Makes about 4 dozen bars.

Plum Pudding Candy

1¼ cups chopped walnuts
1 cup currants *or* raisins
1 cup finely chopped dried figs
¾ cup coarsely chopped dried apricots
½ cup flaked coconut, toasted
3 cups granulated sugar
1 cup milk
1 tablespoon light corn syrup
1 tablespoon butter *or* margarine
1 teaspoon vanilla extract

Butter cookie sheet and side of 3-quart saucepan; set aside. In mixer bowl, combine walnuts, currants, figs, apricots, and toasted coconut; mix well. Set aside.

In prepared saucepan, combine sugar, milk, and corn syrup. Heat and stir over medium heat until sugar is dissolved. Boil gently until mixture reaches 234° (softball stage). Remove from heat. Stir in butter and vanilla. Let stand *without stirring* until cooled to 110°.

Beat for 3 to 4 minutes or until mixture starts to lose its gloss and is satiny in appearance. Quickly stir in fruit mixture. Immediately turn the mixture out onto prepared cookie sheet. Knead with buttered hands until gloss is gone. Divide mixture into four portions. Roll each portion to 14-inch log about 1-inch diameter. Wrap each roll in plastic wrap. Chill 30 minutes, or until firm.

Cut each roll into about ½-inch slices. Place candy pieces in petit four or paper candy cups or wrap individually in clear plastic wrap. Place candies in a box or decorator tin. Securely cover to keep candy fresh.

Makes about 9 dozen pieces.

No-Bake Fudge

1 package (1 pound) confectioners' sugar
2 eggs
1 cup butter *or* margarine
1 package (12 ounces) chocolate pieces
1 teaspoon vanilla extract
1 teaspoon almond extract
1 teaspoon coconut flavoring
½ cup chopped nuts (optional)

Butter 8-inch square baking pan; set aside. In mixer bowl, combine sugar and eggs; mix until shiny and smooth. In small saucepan, melt butter and chocolate pieces over low heat; mix well. Add chocolate mixture to sugar and eggs; blend. Mix in vanilla, almond extract, and coconut flavoring. Stir in nuts, if desired. Pour into prepared pan. Chill; cut into approximately 1¼-inch squares.

Makes 36 pieces.

Variation: Instead of chocolate pieces, use 1 package (12 ounces) peanut butter pieces, 1½ teaspoons vanilla nut extract, and 1 teaspoon caramel flavoring.

Chocolate Mint Truffles

1 package (10 ounces) semisweet chocolate mint-flavored pieces
1 package (6 ounces) semisweet chocolate pieces
1 can (14 ounces) sweetened condensed milk (not evaporated)
  Finely chopped nuts, flaked coconut, chocolate sprinkles, colored sprinkles, unsweetened cocoa *or* colored sugar

In heavy saucepan, melt chocolate mint and semisweet chocolate pieces with sweetened condensed milk over low heat. Chill 2 hours, or until firm. Shape into 1-inch balls; roll in any of the coatings. Chill 1 hour, or until firm. Store in tightly covered container at room temperature.

Makes about 6 dozen.

Variation: In 1-quart glass measure, combine chocolate pieces and sweetened condensed milk. Microwave at HIGH (100% power) 3 minutes, or until chocolate pieces melt, stirring after each 1½ minutes. Stir until smooth. Proceed as above.

Sparkly Cookie Stars

3½ cups all-purpose flour
1 tablespoon baking powder
½ teaspoon salt
1 can (14 ounces) sweetened condensed milk (not evaporated)
¾ cup butter *or* margarine, softened
2 eggs
1 tablespoon vanilla extract *or* 2 teaspoons almond *or* lemon extract
1 egg white, slightly beaten
  Red and green colored sugars

In bowl, combine flour, baking powder, and salt. In large mixer bowl, beat sweetened condensed milk, butter, eggs, and vanilla until well blended. Add flour mixture; mix well. Chill 2 hours. Heat oven to 350°. Grease two cookie sheets. On floured board, knead dough to form a smooth ball. Divide into thirds. On well-floured board, roll out each portion to ⅛-inch thickness. Cut with floured 3-inch star cookie cutter. Reroll as necessary to use all dough. Place 1 inch apart on prepared cookie sheets. Brush with egg white; sprinkle with colored sugars. Bake 7 to 9 minutes, or until lightly browned around edges (*do not overbake*). Cool. Store loosely covered at room temperature.

Makes 6½ dozen cookies.

Black Forest Brownies

 1 package (12 ounces) semisweet chocolate pieces
 ¼ cup butter *or* margarine
 2 cups biscuit baking mix
 1 can (14 ounces) sweetened condensed milk (not evaporated)
 1 egg, beaten
 1 teaspoon almond extract
 ½ cup chopped candied cherries
 ½ cup sliced almonds, toasted

Heat oven to 350°. Generously grease 13x9-inch baking pan. In large saucepan, melt 1 cup chocolate pieces with butter over low heat; remove from heat. Add biscuit mix, sweetened condensed milk, egg, and almond extract. Stir in remaining chocolate pieces and cherries. Turn into prepared baking pan. Top with almonds. Bake 20 to 25 minutes, or until brownies begin to pull away from sides of pan. Cool. Cut into approximately 4x1-inch bars. Store tightly covered at room temperature.

Makes 2 dozen.

Harvest Fruit Conserve

1 cup water
½ cup maple syrup
½ cup dried apples, cut into ½-inch pieces
½ cup dried apricots, cut into quarters
⅓ cup light brown sugar (packed)
1 cup fresh or frozen cranberries
¼ cup chopped walnuts

In saucepan, combine water, maple syrup, apples, apricots and brown sugar; bring to boil. Reduce heat; simmer 10 minutes. Add cranberries; bring to boil. Reduce heat; simmer 5 minutes longer. Stir in walnuts. Cool. Serve as an accompaniment with turkey, chicken, or pork.

Makes about 2 cups.

Curried Rice Mix

1 cup uncooked long-grain rice
4 teaspoons chicken bouillon
1 tablespoon sweet red pepper flakes
1 teaspoon curry powder
¼ teaspoon ground nutmeg

In small bowl, combine rice, bouillon, pepper flakes, curry powder, and nutmeg; mix well. Store in airtight container at room temperature.

Makes about 1 cup.

To Use: In medium saucepan, combine mix and 2½ cups water; bring to boil. Reduce heat; cover and simmer 15 to 20 minutes, or until rice is tender and liquid is absorbed. Stir in ¼ cup toasted slivered almonds and ¼ cup raisins, if desired, just before serving.

Maple Mustard Sauce

1 tablespoon dry mustard
½ teaspoon salt
½ cup half-and-half
½ cup maple syrup
2 egg yolks, beaten
4 teaspoons cider vinegar

In small saucepan, combine mustard and salt. Add 1 tablespoon half-and-half; stir until smooth. Gradually add remaining half-and-half, stirring until smooth. Add maple syrup and egg yolks; mix well. Over medium heat, cook and stir constantly until thick and bubbly. Remove from heat; stir in vinegar. Cool. Serve with ham, pork, or roast beef, or as a dipping sauce for pretzels.

Makes about 1 cup.

Southern-Style Coating Mix

1½ cups dry bread crumbs
4 teaspoons chicken bouillon
1 teaspoon onion powder
1 teaspoon paprika
½ teaspoon garlic powder
½ teaspoon pepper
½ teaspoon dried leaf thyme, crumbled
¼ teaspoon cayenne pepper

In medium bowl, combine crumbs, bouillon, onion powder, paprika, garlic powder, pepper, thyme, and cayenne; mix well. Store in airtight container at room temperature.

Makes about 1½ cups.

To Use: Dip chicken pieces or pork chops in melted butter *or* milk; coat with mix. Bake in preheated 375° oven until tender (about 1 hour for chicken, 35 to 40 minutes for chops).

Maple Barbecue Sauce

½ cup finely chopped onion
2 tablespoons vegetable oil
1 cup maple syrup
⅔ cup bottled chili sauce
3 tablespoons cider vinegar
2 tablespoons prepared mustard
2 teaspoons Worcestershire sauce
½ teaspoon hot pepper sauce

In medium saucepan, cook onion in oil until tender. Add maple syrup, chili sauce, vinegar, mustard, Worcestershire sauce, and pepper sauce; bring to boil. Reduce heat; simmer 5 minutes. Use as a basting sauce for ribs or chicken.

Makes 2⅓ cups.

Herbed Cheese Logs

2 packages (8 ounces each) cream cheese, softened
1 tablespoon milk
2 teaspoons chicken bouillon
½ teaspoon dried leaf basil, crumbled
½ teaspoon dried leaf marjoram, crumbled
½ teaspoon dried leaf oregano, crumbled
½ teaspoon dried leaf thyme, crumbled
¼ teaspoon garlic powder
Cracked black pepper *or* toasted coarsely chopped slivered almonds

In small mixer bowl, beat cream cheese and milk until smooth. Stir in bouillon, basil, marjoram, oregano, thyme, and garlic powder; mix well. Chill 1 hour. Divide cheese mixture in half; place each portion on waxed paper. Shape each into 5-inch log; roll in pepper or almonds. Chill 3 hours, or until firm. Serve with assorted crackers.

Makes about 2 cups.

Three-Bean Soup Mix

¾ cup dry navy beans
⅔ cup dry kidney beans
⅔ cup dry pinto beans
2 tablespoons dry green
    split peas
2 tablespoons dry yellow
    split peas
2 tablespoons beef bouillon
2 tablespoons sweet red *or*
    green pepper flakes
1 tablespoon instant minced
    onion
1 tablespoon celery flakes
2 teaspoons dried leaf thyme,
    crumbled
¼ to ½ teaspoon black pepper

In medium bowl, combine ingredients. Store in airtight container at room temperature.

Makes about 2 cups.

To Use: In large kettle or Dutch oven, brown 1 pound cubed beef, cubed ham, *or* sliced smoked sausage. Add soup mix, 8 cups water and 1 can (14½ ounces) whole tomatoes, undrained and broken up; bring to boil. Reduce heat; cover and simmer 3 hours, or until beans are tender.

Orange Fruitcake Bars

1 can (6 ounces) frozen orange
    juice concentrate, thawed
½ cup plus ⅔ cup light brown
    sugar (packed)
1 cup raisins
1 package (8 ounces) pitted
    dates, chopped
1 jar (1 pound) mixed candied
    fruits, finely chopped
½ cup butter *or* margarine,
    softened
4 eggs
1 cup all-purpose flour
⅛ teaspoon baking soda
½ teaspoon ground cinnamon
½ teaspoon ground nutmeg
¼ teaspoon ground allspice
¼ teaspoon ground cloves
1 cup chopped nuts
    Orange Glaze (follows)
    Candied cherries, halved
    (optional)

Heat oven to 300°. Grease two 15x10-inch jelly roll pans; line with waxed paper; grease paper. In medium saucepan, combine orange juice concentrate and ½ cup brown sugar. Stir over low heat until mixture comes to boil. Add raisins and dates; bring to boil again. Remove from heat, stir in candied fruits, and set aside. In large mixer bowl, cream butter and remaining ⅔ cup sugar until fluffy. Beat in eggs, one at a time. Blend in flour, baking soda, cinnamon, nutmeg, allspice, and cloves. Stir in nuts and fruit mixture. Turn into prepared pans. Bake 35 to 40 minutes, or until cake tester inserted in center comes out clean. Cool. Frost with Orange Glaze. Cut into 3x1-inch bars. Garnish with halved candied cherries, if desired.

Makes 100 bars.

Orange Glaze

1½ cups sifted confectioners'
    sugar
¼ cup orange juice
1 tablespoon butter *or*
    margarine, softened

In small bowl, mix all ingredients until smooth.

Orange Popcorn Balls

4 quarts popped popcorn (about
    ½ cup *plus* 2 tablespoons
    kernels)
1 cup coarsely chopped walnuts
2 cups granulated sugar
½ cup orange juice
½ cup half-and-half
1 tablespoon butter *or*
    margarine
    Grated zest of 1 orange

In large saucepan, combine popcorn and walnuts; set aside. In saucepan, combine sugar, orange juice, and half-and-half; cook over low heat, stirring constantly, until sugar dissolves. Cover and boil 1 minute to dissolve the sugar from the side of pan. Increase the heat slightly and cook, uncovered, to hard ball stage (260°), stirring occasionally. Remove from heat and stir in butter and orange zest. Slowly pour the hot syrup over the popcorn and nuts, tossing until evenly coated. Grease hands with additional butter and shape popcorn mixture into 2-inch balls. The mixture is hot and sets quickly—so work fast. Cool popcorn balls on waxed paper. When cool, wrap in plastic wrap or waxed paper.

Makes 18 to 20 popcorn balls.

Note: This recipe works best with two people—one to pour, the other to stir, and both to quickly form balls.

Orange Macaroon Bars

¼ cup butter *or* margarine, softened
1 cup granulated sugar
1 egg
1 teaspoon grated orange zest
2 tablespoons frozen orange juice concentrate, thawed
1 cup *sifted* all-purpose flour
1 teaspoon baking powder
½ teaspoon salt
1 cup flaked coconut

Heat oven to 350°. Grease 8-inch square baking pan. In medium mixer bowl, cream butter and sugar until fluffy. Beat in egg, orange zest, and orange juice concentrate. Stir in flour, baking powder, salt, and coconut. Spread in prepared pan. Bake 40 to 50 minutes, or until cake tester inserted in center comes out clean. Cool. Cut into 1¼-inch squares.

Makes 36 bars.

Candied Orange Slices

6 oranges
Water
1½ cups dark brown sugar (packed)
2 cups water
Granulated sugar

Place oranges in large saucepan or kettle. Cover with water. Cover and bring to boil over medium heat. Reduce heat and simmer 40 minutes, or until zest is tender. Drain and cool. Cut oranges in ⅜-inch crosswise slices and cut slices in half; place in bowl. In medium saucepan, mix together brown sugar and water. Stir over low heat until sugar dissolves and mixture comes to boil. Boil, stirring frequently, 20 minutes, or until thick and syrupy. Pour over orange slices. Cover and chill 8 hours, or overnight. Remove orange slices from

syrup and roll in sugar; place on rack to dry overnight. Roll in sugar again just before packing in gift boxes.

Makes about 6 cups.

Fabulous Orange Fudge

2 cups granulated sugar
1 can (5⅓ ounces) evaporated milk (not sweetened condensed)
10 large *or* 100 miniature marshmallows
1 package (6 ounces) semisweet chocolate pieces
1 cup chopped walnuts
½ cup butter *or* margarine, cut into small pieces
Grated zest of 2 oranges

Butter 8-inch square baking pan. In saucepan, combine sugar, evaporated milk, and marshmallows. Bring to boil over medium heat, stirring to dissolve the sugar. Boil 6 minutes, stirring constantly. Remove from heat. Add chocolate, walnuts, butter, and orange zest. Beat well 5 minutes, until fudge thickens. Pour into prepared baking pan. Chill until firm. Cut into 1¾-inch squares.

Makes 25 pieces.

Orange Chocolate Balls

2 boxes (8½ ounces each) chocolate wafers, crushed (4 cups)
1 cup confectioners' sugar
⅓ cup frozen concentrate for orange juice, thawed
¼ cup light corn syrup
¼ cup butter *or* margarine, melted
1 cup finely chopped walnuts
Confectioners' sugar for dusting

In large bowl, combine cookie crumbs, sugar, orange juice concentrate, corn syrup, butter, and walnuts; mix well. Shape into 1-inch balls. Chill 3 hours. Roll in confectioners' sugar just before packing in gift containers.

Makes 4 dozen cookies.

1000 Palms Stuffed Dates

4 dozen dates
2½ cups confectioners' sugar
½ cup sweetened condensed milk (not evaporated)
Grated zest of 1 lemon
½ cup finely chopped walnuts *or* pecans
¼ cup finely chopped dried apricots
Walnut *or* pecan quarters *or* halves (optional)

To prepare the dates for stuffing, cut each date along one side and remove pits. In bowl, combine confectioners' sugar, sweetened condensed milk, and lemon zest (mixture will be stiff). Stir in chopped nuts and apricots. Dust hands with additional confectioners' sugar and shape mixture into ¾-inch balls; stuff into prepared dates. Top each with a nut quarter or half.

Makes 4 dozen.

Western Golden Fruitcake

1 cup butter *or* margarine, softened
2 cups granulated sugar
4 eggs
4 cups all-purpose flour
1½ teaspoons baking soda
1 cup buttermilk
½ cup orange juice
2 cups pecan *or* walnut halves
1 package (8 ounces) pitted dates, chopped
8 ounces candied cherries, halved
8 ounces candied pineapple chunks
Grated zest of 2 oranges
Fresh Orange *or* Lemon Glaze (follows)
Nut halves (optional)

Heat oven to 300°. Generously grease 10-inch Bundt or tube pan *and* 7½x3½-inch loaf pan. In large mixer bowl, cream butter and sugar until light and fluffy. Beat in eggs one at a time. Sift flour and baking soda. Add to creamed mixture alternately with buttermilk and orange juice, beating until smooth. Stir in nuts, dates, cherries, pineapple, and orange zest. Spoon 7½ cups of batter into prepared Bundt or tube pan and spoon remaining 2½ cups of batter into prepared loaf pan. Bake both cakes 2 hours, or until a wooden pick inserted in center comes out clean. Cool 10 minutes. Remove from pans and cool on wire racks. To serve, drizzle cakes with Fresh Orange or Lemon Glaze and garnish with nut halves, if desired.

Large cake makes 12 to 16 servings and small loaf 4 to 6 servings.

Fresh Orange Glaze

1 cup confectioners' sugar
2 tablespoons orange juice
1 teaspoon grated orange zest

In small bowl, combine sugar, orange juice, and orange zest.

Fresh Lemon Glaze

1 cup confectioners' sugar
2 tablespoons lemon juice
1 teaspoon grated lemon zest

In small bowl, combine sugar, lemon juice, and lemon zest.

Candied Citrus Peel

4 to 5 oranges *or* 6 lemons *or* 2 grapefruits
12 cups cold water
2 cups granulated sugar
½ cup honey
1¾ cups boiling water

Score citrus in quarters and remove sections of peel. Cut into uniform strips about ⅜ inch wide to yield 3 cups peel. (Save peeled fruit for other uses.) In large saucepan, bring 6 cups cold water and peel to a boil; boil 10 minutes. Drain and rinse. Repeat process with 6 cups fresh cold water. In same saucepan, bring to boil 1½ cups of sugar, honey, and boiling water, stirring to dissolve sugar; boil 1 minute. Add drained peel and simmer briskly 40 to 45 minutes, stirring frequently to avoid sticking. Drain well. In large bowl, toss drained peel with remaining ½ cup sugar to coat well. Spread on waxed paper to dry. Store in tightly covered container.

Makes 1 pound.

Chocolate Dipped Candied Citrus Peel

6 ounces sweet chocolate or white sweet chocolate
1 pound Candied Citrus Peel (preceding)

In top of double boiler, over hot (not boiling) water, melt chocolate; stir occasionally. Dip each piece Candied Citrus Peel in chocolate, covering one half to two thirds of each piece only; gently shake off any excess chocolate. Cool on waxed paper until chocolate is set.

Variation: Substitute semisweet chocolate pieces and 2 teaspoons vegetable shortening for sweet chocolate, melting chocolate pieces with shortening.

White Citrus Fudge

2 tablespoons butter *or* margarine
2 cups granulated sugar
¾ cup milk
Grated zest of 1 lemon *or* orange
½ cup chopped walnuts

In saucepan, melt butter over medium-low heat. Add sugar and milk, stirring to dissolve sugar. Cover and boil 1 minute to dissolve sugar from sides of pan. Cook, uncovered, without stirring, to soft-ball stage (239°). Cool to lukewarm, about 45 minutes, without stirring. Add lemon zest. Beat vigorously until mixture loses its glossiness and is ready to set. Stir in walnuts and pour immediately onto waxed paper. Cool and cut into squares.

Makes about 1 pound.

Note: Do not make this fudge on rainy or very humid days.

Teddy Bear Gift Bread
(Shown on page 125)

1½ cups all-purpose flour
½ cup whole-wheat flour
½ cup light brown sugar
(packed)
¾ cup granulated sugar
3 teaspoons baking powder
¼ teaspoon baking soda
½ teaspoon salt
1 teaspoon pumpkin pie spice
½ teaspoon ground cinnamon
¼ teaspoon ground ginger
1 egg, beaten
1 cup lowfat milk
1½ tablespoons vegetable oil
Candy to decorate

Heat oven to 350° Generously grease or spray Teddy Bear baking pan with non-stick cooking spray. In food processor or large bowl, mix flours, sugars, baking powder, baking soda, salt, pumpkin pie spice, cinnamon, and ginger. Add egg, milk, and oil. Mix until *just* blended. Bake 20 to 25 minutes, or until knife inserted comes out clean. Let cool and then remove bread from pan onto flat surface.

To Decorate: Use jelly beans for eyes, a nonpareil for nose, red shoe string licorice for mouth, black shoe string licorice for bowtie, and jelly beans for buttons.

To Microwave: Use microwave Teddy Bear baking pan. Generously grease or spray baking pan with non-stick cooking spray. Microwave on MEDIUM (50% power) 1 minute. Turn. Microwave 2 minutes 30 seconds at HIGH (100% power), stopping to turn once. Microwave on MEDIUM 3 minutes, or until knife inserted comes out clean. Cool and then remove from pan.

Spiced Banana Cookie Wreath

2 extra-ripe, medium bananas, peeled
2 cups granola
1½ cups all-purpose flour
1 cup light brown sugar
(packed)
1 teaspoon baking powder
1 teaspoon ground cinnamon
½ teaspoon ground nutmeg
¼ teaspoon salt
1 egg
½ cup butter *or* margarine, melted
¼ cup vegetable oil
1 cup raisins
⅓ cup chopped almonds
½ cup confectioners' sugar
1 tablespoon milk
Candied cherries (optional)
Red and green colored sugars
(optional)

Heat oven to 375°. Grease three cookie sheets. Puree bananas in blender to measure 1 cup. In mixer bowl, combine granola, flour, brown sugar, baking powder, cinnamon, nutmeg, and salt. Beat in bananas, egg, butter, and oil. Stir in raisins. For each of 3 wreaths, drop dough by generous teaspoonfuls onto prepared cookie sheets in a circle. Spoonfuls of dough should be *just* touching. Sprinkle with almonds. Bake 15 to 18 minutes, until lightly browned. Cool on cookie sheets. In bowl, mix sugar and milk until smooth. Drizzle over cooled wreaths. Decorate with candied cherries or colored sugars, if desired. Tie with a bow to give as a gift.

Makes 3 wreaths, 16 cookies per wreath.

Caroler's Rewards

Greet the carolers with cups of good cheer and sweet treats. Fireside Punch, white Hot Chocolate, Cranberry Walnut Crescents and Glazed Pound Cake are all sure to please.

Fresh Fruit Tray

- 1 fresh pineapple
- 2 medium bananas
- 2 cups whole strawberries
  Crisp salad greens
  Latin Lime Dunk (follows)

Twist crown from pineapple; cut pineapple in half lengthwise. Cut fruit from shells; core and chunk fruit. Peel and slice bananas. Arrange pineapple, bananas and strawberries on platter lined with salad greens. Make Latin Lime Dunk and serve with fruit.

Makes 6 servings.

Latin Lime Dunk

- 1 package (3 ounces) cream cheese, softened
- 3 tablespoons confectioners' sugar
- ¼ teaspoon grated lime zest
- 1 tablespoon lime juice
- ¼ cup heavy cream, whipped

In small mixer bowl, beat cream cheese, confectioners' sugar, lime zest, and juice until smooth. Gradually fold in cream.

Mandarin Orange Yogurt Tart

- Gingersnap Crust (follows)
- 2 cans (11 ounces each) mandarin orange sections
- 4 teaspoons unflavored gelatine
- 2 containers (8 ounces each) vanilla lowfat yogurt
- 1 tablespoon granulated sugar (optional)
- 1 tablespoon grated orange zest
- 1 teaspoon cornstarch

Prepare Gingersnap Crust; set aside. Drain mandarin oranges; reserve 1½ cups syrup. (If necessary, add orange juice to measure 1½ cups liquid.) Pour 1 cup syrup into small saucepan. Sprinkle gelatine over. Heat and stir until gelatin dissolves. Cool 10 minutes. Stir in yogurt, sugar, if desired, and orange zest. Chill until mixture thickens slightly. Pour into Gingersnap Crust. Chill 4 hours, or overnight.

Crust. Chill 4 hours, or overnight.

Arrange oranges on top. In a saucepan, combine remaining ½ cup syrup with cornstarch. Cook, stirring, until boiling and thickened. Cool. Spoon over oranges.

Makes 8 servings.

Gingersnap Crust

- 1½ cups gingersnap cookie crumbs
- 3 tablespoons butter *or* margarine, melted

In small bowl, combine crumbs and melted butter. Press in 9-inch tart pan with removable bottom.

113

Glazed Pound Cake

1 package (2-layer size) lemon cake mix
1 package (4-serving size) lemon flavor gelatin
¾ cup water
¼ cup vegetable oil
4 eggs
Easy Lemon Glaze (follows)
Large red gumdrops (optional)

Heat oven to 350°. Line bottom of 10-inch tube pan with waxed paper. In large mixer bowl, combine cake mix, gelatin, water, oil, and eggs. Blend at low speed just to moisten. Increase speed to medium and beat 3 minutes until creamy. Pour into prepared pan. Bake 50 minutes, or until cake springs back when lightly pressed. Cool in pan 15 minutes.

Turn out onto wire rack. Make Easy Lemon Glaze; poke holes in warm cake with wooden pick and slowly pour on glaze. Chill. Decorate with flattened gumdrops, cut to resemble poinsettia petals, if desired.

Easy Lemon Glaze
⅓ cup lemon juice
2 cups sifted confectioners' sugar
2 tablespoons butter *or* margarine, melted
1 tablespoon water

Gradually add lemon juice to sugar in bowl. Blend until smooth. Stir in butter and water until smooth.

Makes 1¼ cups.

SPECIAL HINTS

In high altitude areas, add ¾ cup all-purpose flour, increase water to 1½ cups, and reduce oil to 2 tablespoons; bake at 375°.

Gelatin Poke Cake

1 package (2-layer size) white cake mix
1 package (4-serving size) gelatin, any flavor
1 cup boiling water
½ cup cold water
1 container (8 ounces) non-dairy whipped topping, thawed
Sliced fresh fruit (optional)
Marzipan (follows) (optional)

Heat oven to 350°. Generously grease and flour 13x9-inch pan. Prepare cake batter as directed on package, and pour into prepared pan. Bake 30 minutes, or until cake tester inserted in center comes out clean. Cool cake in pan 15 minutes, then pierce with utility fork at ½-inch intervals.

Meanwhile, dissolve gelatin in boiling water. Add cold water and carefully pour over cake. Chill 3 to 4 hours. Garnish with whipped topping and fruit or Marzipan, if desired.

Marzipan

1¾ cups flaked coconut, finely chopped
1 package (4-serving size) gelatin, any flavor
1 cup ground blanched almonds
⅔ cup sweetened condensed milk (not evaporated)
1½ teaspoons granulated sugar
1 teaspoon almond extract
Food coloring (optional)
Whole cloves, citron, angelica (optional)

In large bowl, thoroughly mix coconut, gelatin, almonds, condensed milk, sugar, and almond extract. Shape by hand into small fruits, vegetables, hearts, Easter eggs, or other forms. (Or use small candy molds). If desired, use food coloring to paint details on fruit; add whole cloves and citron or angelica for stems and blossom-ends. Chill until dry. Store in covered container at room temperature.

Makes 3 cups or 2 to 3 dozen confections.

Variations
Fruits: Use strawberry flavor gelatin for strawberries; lemon flavor gelatin for bananas, grapefruit, lemons, Bartlett pears; lime flavor gelatin for green apples or pears, leaves, stems, limes; orange flavor gelatin for carrots, pumpkins, tangerines, oranges; cherry or black cherry flavor gelatin for cherries; grape flavor for grapes.

Birds: Add enough food coloring to marzipan mixture to tint deep red or yellow. For each bird, shape body, head, and tail in one piece, starting with a 1- to 1½-inch ball of the mixture. Press on two small pieces to form wings. Use 2 poppy seeds for eyes and one chocolate sprinkle for a beak. Attach to cake.

Cranberry Walnut Crescents

- 1 **can (16 ounces) whole berry cranberry sauce**
- 2 **teaspoons cornstarch**
- 1½ **cups chopped toasted walnuts**
- 1 **cup butter *or* margarine, softened**
- 1 **cup granulated sugar**
- 3 **eggs**
- 2 **teaspoons vanilla extract**
- 1 **tablespoon water**
- 4¼ **cups all-purpose flour**
- 1 **package (6 ounces) semisweet chocolate pieces**
- 2 **teaspoons vegetable shortening**

In saucepan, blend cranberry sauce and cornstarch; stir constantly over medium heat until mixture boils 1 minute. Remove from heat; cool. Stir in ½ cup walnuts; set aside.

In large mixer bowl, cream butter and sugar until light and fluffy. Separate 1 egg; add egg white and remaining 2 eggs to creamed mixture, beating until light and fluffy. Add vanilla. In small bowl, beat egg yolk with water; set aside. Gradually blend flour into creamed mixture; cover and chill dough 1 hour.

Heat oven to 350°. Lightly grease two cookie sheets. On lightly floured board, roll out dough, half at a time, to ⅛-inch thickness. With cookie cutter, cut into 3-inch circles. To form each cookie, place about 1 teaspoon cranberry filling onto 1 side of dough circle; brush edges of cookies with water. Fold over dough to encase filling and form a crescent shape. Gently press edges of cookie together with tines

of fork. Place on prepared cookie sheets. Brush lightly with egg yolk mixture. Bake 12 minutes, or until edges are light brown. Cool on wire rack.

In saucepan, melt chocolate with shortening over low heat, stirring constantly. Remove from heat; cool 3 minutes, or until slightly thickened. Dip ends of cookies into chocolate glaze; sprinkle with remaining walnuts. Let cookies stand until chocolate is firm. Store cookies in airtight container in refrigerator. Bring to room temperature before serving.

Makes 4 dozen.

Cranberry Apple Tea

- 3 **cups cranberry apple drink**
- 1 **cinnamon stick**
- 2 **teaspoons honey**
  Dash ground ginger
- 2 **tea bags**
  Apple slices (optional)
  Cinnamon sticks (optional)

In saucepan, heat cranberry apple drink, cinnamon stick, honey, and ginger *just* to boiling. Remove from heat and add tea bags. Cover; let stand 5 minutes. Remove tea bags and cinnamon stick. Pour into mugs and serve hot with apple slices and cinnamon sticks, if desired.

Makes 4 servings.

Cranberry Nut Roll

- 4 eggs, separated
- ½ cup granulated sugar
- ½ cup finely chopped walnuts
- 1 cup chopped cranberries
- ⅓ cup *sifted* cake flour
- 2 tablespoons cornstarch
- 1 teaspoon ground cinnamon
- 2 tablespoons butter *or* margarine, melted
  Confectioners' sugar
- 2 foil-wrapped (4 ounces) white baking bars
- 1 cup heavy cream
  White Buttercream (follows)

Heat oven to 350°. Grease 15x10-inch jelly roll pan; line with waxed paper; grease paper. In large mixer bowl, beat egg whites until foamy. Gradually add ¼ cup sugar; beat until stiff peaks form; set aside. In small mixer bowl, beat egg yolks and remaining ¼ cup sugar 3 minutes, or until light and fluffy. Fold in walnuts, cranberries, flour, cornstarch, and cinnamon; gently fold into egg white mixture. Fold in melted butter. Spread batter in prepared pan. Bake 20 minutes, or until top springs back when lightly pressed. Loosen cake from pan; cool 10 minutes. Invert cake onto cloth towel sprinkled with confectioners' sugar. Peel off waxed paper. Starting from narrow side, roll up warm cake. Cool cake, seam-side down, on wire rack.

In top of double boiler, over hot (not boiling) water, combine white baking bars and 2 tablespoons cream; stir until baking bars are melted and mixture is smooth. In small mixer bowl, combine melted mixture and remaining cream. Chill. Beat cream mixture *just* until soft peaks form.

Unroll cooled cake. Spread whipped cream mixture evenly over cake to within ½-inch of edges; roll up cake. Pipe or spread White Buttercream over cake. Refrigerate until ready to serve.

Makes 10 to 12 servings.

White Buttercream

- 1 package (6 ounces) white baking bars, broken up
- ¼ cup heavy cream
- 1 cup cold butter *or* margarine, cut into pieces
- 1 cup confectioners' sugar

In top of double boiler, over hot (not boiling) water, heat baking bars and cream, stirring until baking bars are melted and mixture is smooth. Transfer to large mixer bowl; cool to room temperature.

Gradually beat in cold butter and confectioners' sugar; beat until light and fluffy.

Makes 3 cups.

Hot White Chocolate

- 1 cup chopped white deluxe baking pieces
- 4 cups milk
- ¼ cup almond-flavored liqueur
- ½ cup heavy cream, whipped

In large saucepan, combine ⅔ cup baking pieces and milk. Stir over medium heat until baking pieces are melted and mixture is hot but *not boiling*. Remove from heat; add liqueur.

Pour into 4 heat-proof mugs. Serve hot, topped with whipped cream and sprinkled with remaining chopped baking pieces.

Makes four 1-cup servings.

117

Pistachio Truffle Pie

Pistachio Crumb Crust
(follows)
½ cup light corn syrup
1 package (6 ounces)
    semisweet chocolate pieces
2 teaspoons instant coffee
    powder *or* 2 tablespoons
    coffee-flavored liqueur
3 egg yolks, beaten
2 cups heavy cream
1 tablespoon granulated sugar
¼ teaspoon vanilla extract
1¼ cups coarsely chopped
    pistachios
    Chocolate curls

Make Pistachio Crumb Crust; set aside. In small saucepan, combine corn syrup, chocolate pieces, and instant coffee over low heat; stir until chocolate is melted and mixture is smooth. Cool. Stir in egg yolks; mix thoroughly. In mixer bowl, beat 1½ cups cream until soft peaks form; gradually fold cream and ¾ cup pistachios into chocolate mixture. Spoon into prepared crust. Chill at least 2 hours. Beat remaining cream, sugar, and vanilla; use to garnish top, along with chocolate curls and remaining ½ cup pistachios.

Makes 10 to 12 servings.

Pistachio Crumb Crust

¾ cup vanilla wafer crumbs
⅓ cup granulated sugar
¼ cup chopped pistachios
¼ cup butter *or* margarine,
    melted
2 tablespoons unsweetened
    cocoa

Heat oven to 375°. In small bowl, combine crumbs, sugar, pistachios, butter, and cocoa. Press into 9-inch pie plate. Bake 7 to 9 minutes, or until firm. Cool.

Pumpkin Cheesecake Bavarian

Pumpkin layer

1½ cups solid pack pumpkin
½ cup sour cream
2 egg yolks
½ teaspoon ground nutmeg
½ teaspoon ground ginger
⅛ teaspoon ground cloves
¾ cup granulated sugar
4 egg whites
1 cup gingersnap crumbs
¼ cup butter *or* margarine,
    melted

Cheesecake layer

Spiced whipped cream
2 egg yolks
½ cup sour cream
⅓ cup granulated sugar
1 tablespoon all-purpose flour
½ teaspoon vanilla extract
1 package (8 ounces) cream
    cheese, softened

Heat oven to 325°. Grease 9-inch springform pan. In large bowl, combine pumpkin, sour cream, yolks, nutmeg, ginger, cloves, and ¼ cup of sugar; mix well. In large mixer bowl, beat egg yolks, gradually adding remaining ½ cup sugar; beat until stiff peaks form. Fold into pumpkin mixture. Pour into prepared pan. In small bowl, mix gingersnap crumbs and butter; top pumpkin layer with crumbs.

In mixer bowl, beat yolks until pale. Blend in sour cream, sugar, flour, and vanilla. Beat in cream cheese until smooth. Pour over gingersnap crumbs. Bake 55 minutes, or until set. Chill. Garnish with dollops of spiced whipped cream.

Makes 10 to 12 servings.

Season's Greetings Punch

    3 quarts pineapple juice, chilled
    2 cans (6 ounces each) frozen
        limeade concentrate,
        thawed
    2 quarts ginger ale, chilled
    2 pints strawberry sorbet
        Strawberries, pineapple
        chunks, or orange slices

Pour pineapple juice and limeade concentrate into punch bowl to blend. Just before serving, add ginger ale and scoops of sorbet. Garnish with strawberries, pineapple chunks, or orange slices.

Makes 50 four-ounce servings.

Raspberry Melody Punch

    2 bottles (40 ounces each)
        raspberry juice, chilled
    1 package (12 ounces) frozen
        raspberries, thawed
    2 cans (12 ounces each) lemon-
        lime soda, chilled
    1 cup fresh mint sprigs
    1 orange, thinly sliced

In punch bowl, combine juice, raspberries, and soda. Float mint and orange on top.

Makes 18 servings.

Hot Orchard Peach Cup

    1 bottle (40 ounces) peach juice
    ¼ cup light brown sugar
        (packed)
    2 cinnamon sticks
    2 tablespoons butter or
        margarine
    ½ cup peach schnapps (optional)

In Dutch oven, combine juice, brown sugar, cinnamon, and butter. Heat to boil. Remove from heat. Add schnapps, if desired. Serve hot.

Makes 6 servings.

Hot Orange Cranberry Punch

    2 cups orange juice
    2 cups cranberry juice cocktail
    2 cups very strong tea
    ⅓ cup granulated sugar
    ¼ teaspoon ground nutmeg
    ¼ teaspoon ground cinnamon
        Orange cartwheels (optional)
        Whole cloves (optional)

In Dutch oven, combine juices, tea, sugar, nutmeg, and cinnamon; heat to *just* under boiling. Pour into heat-proof serving bowl; keep hot. Garnish with unpeeled orange cartwheels studded with whole cloves, if desired.

Hot Pineapple Port Cup

    6 cups pineapple juice
    1 bottle (750 ml) port wine
    1 cup raisins
    ½ cup granulated sugar
        Zest from 1 orange

In Dutch oven or large kettle, combine juice, wine, raisins, sugar, and orange zest. Heat to boiling; reduce heat and simmer 15 minutes. Serve hot.

Makes 12 servings.

Paradise Fruit Nog

    2 tablespoons butter or
        margarine
    ½ cup light brown sugar
        (packed)
    1 cup whole almonds, lightly
        toasted
    1 cup raisins
    ½ teaspoon ground cinnamon
    6 cups pineapple juice

In Dutch oven, melt butter. Stir in brown sugar until blended. Stir in almonds, raisins, and cinnamon. Gradually stir in pineapple juice. Heat to simmer for 15 minutes. Serve hot.

Makes 8 servings.

Fireside Punch

    1½ cups cranberry juice cocktail
    1½ cups cold water
      4 cinnamon apple or orange
          herbal tea bags
      2 tablespoons light brown
          sugar (packed)
          Cinnamon sticks (optional)
          Fresh cranberries (optional)

In 1-quart glass measure, combine cranberry juice, water, and herbal tea bags. Microwave on HIGH (100% power) 6 minutes, or until very hot. (*Mixture should not boil.*) Let stand 5 minutes. Remove tea bags; stir in brown sugar. Pour into mugs and garnish with cinnamon sticks and cranberries, if desired.

Makes 5 servings.

CONVENTIONAL DIRECTIONS

In medium saucepan, bring cranberry juice and water to boil. Add herbal tea bags; cover and brew 5 minutes. Remove tea bags; stir in sugar. Serve as above.

Christmas Sled

Oh, for the winters that used to be!
The winters that only a boy may see!
Rich with the snowflakes' rush and swirl,
Keen as a diamond, pure as a pearl,
Brimming with healthful, rollicking fun,
Sweet with their rest when the play was done,
With kindly revels each day decreed,
And a Christmas sled for the royal steed.

Down from the crest with shrill hurray!
Clear the track, there! Out of the way!
Scarcely touching the path beneath,
Scarce admitting of breath to breathe,
Dashing along, with leap and swerve,
Over the crossing, round the curve.
Talk of your flying machines! Instead,
Give me the swoop of that Christmas sled.

AUTHOR UNKNOWN

Sweet Temptation Cookies

Christmas Candy Cane Cookies, Moist & Minty Brownies and Chocolate Pecan Pie Bars are just a few of the deliciously tempting cookies you'll find here. A splendid selection for moments of indulgence.

Chocolate Cherry-Nut Drops

  2/3 cup butter *or* margarine,
       softened
    1 cup granulated sugar
    1 egg
    1 teaspoon vanilla extract
1 3/4 cups all-purpose flour
  1/2 cup unsweetened cocoa
  1/2 teaspoon baking soda
  1/4 teaspoon salt
  1/3 cup water
  1/2 cup chopped nuts
  1/3 cup finely chopped
       maraschino cherries,
       well drained
       Vanilla Glaze (follows)
       Multicolored sprinkles
       (optional)

Heat oven to 350°. In large mixer bowl, cream butter and sugar until light and fluffy. Add egg and vanilla, blending well. Mix flour, cocoa, baking soda, and salt; add alternately with water to creamed mixture. Stir in nuts and maraschino cherries. Cover; chill until firm, about 1 hour. Drop by heaping teaspoonfuls onto ungreased cookie sheet. Bake 8 to 10 minutes, or until set. Cool 1 minute; remove from cookie sheet to wire rack. Cool completely. Prepare Vanilla Glaze. Drizzle over top of drops in a random pattern. Garnish with sprinkles, if desired.

Makes about 3 1/2 dozen cookies.

Vanilla Glaze

    1 tablespoon butter *or* margarine
    1 cup confectioners' sugar
1 to 2 tablespoons hot water
  1/4 teaspoon vanilla extract
  1/8 teaspoon almond extract

In small saucepan over low heat, melt butter. Add confectioners' sugar alternately with water, vanilla, and almond extract, beating with wire whisk until smooth.

Filled Slice 'N Bake Chocolate Cookies

  3/4 cup butter *or* margarine,
       softened
    1 cup granulated sugar
    1 egg
    1 teaspoon vanilla extract
1 3/4 cups all-purpose flour
  2/3 cup unsweetened cocoa
    1 teaspoon baking powder
  1/2 teaspoon baking soda
  1/2 teaspoon salt
    3 tablespoons milk
       Creamy Filling (follows)

In large mixer bowl, beat butter and sugar until blended. Add egg and vanilla; beat well. Mix flour, cocoa, baking powder, baking soda, and salt; add to butter mixture alternately with milk, beating until well blended. Cover; chill 1 hour, or until firm enough to handle. Turn dough onto lightly floured board. Divide in half. With hands, shape each half into a roll 7 1/2 inches long. Wrap each in aluminum foil; freeze about 8 hours.

Heat oven to 325°. Lightly grease cookie sheet. With sharp knife, cut rolls into 1/8-inch slices. Place about 1 inch apart on prepared cookie sheet. Bake 9 to 10 minutes, or until firm. Cool 1 minute. Remove to wire rack; cool completely. Make Creamy Filling. Put cookies together, sandwich style, with filling. Garnish one side of cookie with small amount of filling placed in pastry bag fitted with small star tip.

Makes about 4 dozen filled cookies.

Creamy Filling

    1 package (3 ounces) cream
       cheese, softened
    1 tablespoon butter *or*
       margarine, softened
2 1/4 cups confectioners' sugar
    1 teaspoon milk
  1/2 teaspoon vanilla extract
    4 to 5 drops red food coloring
       (optional)
  1/8 teaspoon peppermint extract
       (optional)

In small mixer bowl, beat cream cheese and butter until blended. Gradually add confectioners' sugar and milk, beating until smooth. Blend in vanilla, food coloring, and peppermint extract, if desired.

Makes about 1 1/4 cups filling.

Cocoa Sandies

    1 cup butter *or* margarine,
       softened
1 1/4 cups confectioners' sugar
1 1/2 teaspoons vanilla extract
  1/2 cup unsweetened cocoa
1 3/4 cups all-purpose flour
       Chocolate Glaze (follows)

Heat oven to 300°. In large mixer bowl, beat butter, confectioners' sugar, and vanilla until creamy. Add cocoa; blend well. Gradually add flour, blending until smooth. On lightly floured board or between two pieces of waxed paper, roll dough to about 1/2-inch thickness. Cut dough into heart or star shapes with 2 1/2-inch cookie cutters. (Scraps can be gathered and rerolled.) Place on ungreased cookie sheet. Bake 20 minutes, or just until firm. Cool slightly; remove from cookie sheet to wire rack. Cool completely. Make Chocolate Glaze. Dip about half of each cookie into glaze. Place on wire rack until glaze is set.

Makes 2 dozen cookies.

Chocolate Glaze

    3 tablespoons butter *or*
        margarine
    ⅓ cup unsweetened cocoa
    ¼ cup water
    1 teaspoon vanilla extract
    1½ cups confectioners' sugar

In small saucepan, melt butter over low heat. Stir in cocoa and water. Cook over low heat, stirring constantly, until mixture thickens; do not boil. Remove from heat; stir in vanilla. Gradually add confectioners' sugar, stirring with wire whisk until smooth. Add additional water, 1 teaspoon at a time, if needed, for desired consistency.

Chocolate Pecan Pie Bars

    1⅓ cups all-purpose flour
    ½ cup plus 2 tablespoons light
        brown sugar (packed)
    ½ cup butter *or*
        margarine
    2 eggs
    ½ cup light corn syrup
    ¼ cup unsweetened cocoa
    2 tablespoons butter *or*
        margarine, melted
    1 teaspoon vanilla extract
    ⅛ teaspoon salt
    1 cup coarsely chopped pecans

Heat oven to 350°. In medium bowl, mix flour and 2 tablespoons brown sugar. Using pastry blender or two knives, cut in ½ cup butter until mixture resembles coarse crumbs; press onto bottom and about 1 inch up sides of 9-inch square baking pan. Bake 10 to 12 minutes, or until set. With back of spoon, lightly press crust into corners and against sides of pan.

Meanwhile, in small bowl, lightly beat eggs, corn syrup, remaining ½ cup brown sugar, cocoa, melted butter, vanilla, and salt. Stir in pecans. Pour mixture over warm crust. Bake 25 minutes, or until pecan filling is set. Cool. Cut into approximately 1x4 inch bars.

Makes about 16 bars.

Almond Orange Dainties

    Chocolate Filling (follows)
    1½ cups butter *or* margarine,
        softened
    ¾ cup granulated sugar
    1½ teaspoons vanilla extract
    3 egg yolks
    3 cups all-purpose flour
    ¾ teaspoon baking powder
    ½ teaspoon salt
    2 to 3 teaspoons grated orange
        zest
    1 cup toasted sliced almonds,
        ground

Heat oven to 325°. Prepare Chocolate Filling; refrigerate. In large mixer bowl, beat butter, sugar, vanilla, and egg yolks until creamy. Mix flour, baking powder, and salt; gradually add to butter mixture, blending well. Stir in orange zest. Cover; chill about 1 hour, or until firm enough to handle. Shape dough into 1-inch balls; roll in ground almonds. Place about 2 inches apart on ungreased cookie sheet. Press thumb in center of each cookie; place about ¼ teaspoon filling in each thumbprint. Bake 11 to 13 minutes, or until set. Cool slightly; remove from cookie sheet to wire rack. Cool completely.

Makes 5 dozen cookies.

Chocolate Filling

    ⅓ cup granulated sugar
    ¼ cup unsweetened cocoa
    1 tablespoon all-purpose flour
    ½ cup heavy cream
    1 egg yolk, slightly beaten
    2 tablespoons butter *or*
        margarine
    ½ teaspoon vanilla extract

In small saucepan, combine sugar, cocoa, and flour. Gradually stir in heavy cream. Cook over low heat, stirring constantly, until mixture boils. Blend small amount hot mixture into egg yolk. Return to saucepan; blend well. Cook and stir 1 minute. Remove from heat. Add butter and vanilla; stir until mixture is smooth. Refrigerate until ready to use.

To toast almonds: Toast in shallow baking pan in 350° oven, stirring occasionally, 8 to 10 minutes, or until golden brown.

Christmas Stained Glass Cookies

    Colored hard candies
        (about ⅓ cup)
    ¾ cup butter *or* margarine,
        softened
    ¾ cup granulated sugar
    2 eggs
    1 teaspoon vanilla extract
    3 cups all-purpose flour
    1 teaspoon baking powder
    Frosting (optional)
    Candy (optional)

Separate colors of hard candy. Put each color of candy in a freezer bag and crush with a wooden mallet. Set crushed candy aside. In a large mixer bowl, cream butter and sugar until light and fluffy. Beat in eggs and vanilla. In a large bowl, sift flour and baking powder. Gradually stir flour mixture into creamed mixture until dough is very stiff. Wrap in plastic wrap and chill until firm, about 3 hours.

Heat oven to 375°. Line cookie sheet with aluminum foil. On lightly floured board, roll out dough to ⅛-inch thickness. (Additional flour can be added if necessary.) Cut out cookies using large Christmas cookie cutters. Transfer cookies to a prepared cookie sheet. Using a small Christmas cookie cutter of the same shape as the large one, cut out and remove dough from center of each cookie. Fill cutout sections with crushed candy. If using cookies as hanging ornaments, make holes with a chopstick at the top of cookies for string. Bake 7 to 9 minutes, or until cookies are lightly browned and the candy is melted. Slide foil off cookie sheets. When cool, carefully loosen cookies from foil. If desired, decorate with frosting and candy.

Makes about 2½ dozen cookies.

Lemon Nut Cookies

- 1½ **cups all-purpose flour**
- ¾ **teaspoon baking soda**
- ½ **teaspoon salt**
- ¾ **cup butter _or_ margarine, softened**
- ½ **cup light or dark brown sugar (packed)**
- ¼ **cup granulated sugar**
- 1 **egg**
- 1 **tablespoon lemon juice**
- 1 **package (10 ounces) white deluxe baking pieces**
- 1 **cup coarsely chopped cashews or walnuts**
- 1 **teaspoon grated lemon zest**

Heat oven to 375°. In small bowl, mix flour, baking soda and salt; set aside. In large mixer bowl, beat butter and sugars until creamy. Beat in egg and lemon juice; gradually blend in flour mixture. Stir in white baking pieces, nuts, and lemon zest. Drop, by heaping tablespoonfuls onto ungreased cookie sheets. Bake 7 to 10 minutes, or until edges are lightly browned. Cool 2 minutes. Remove to wire racks; cool completely.

Makes 2½ dozen cookies.

Christmas Candy Cane Cookies

- 1 **cup butter _or_ margarine, softened**
- ¾ **cup granulated sugar**
- 1 **egg**
- 1 **teaspoon vanilla extract**
- 1 **teaspoon almond extract**
- 2½ **cups all-purpose flour**
- ¼ **teaspoon red food coloring**
- ¼ **teaspoon green food coloring Sugar**

In large mixer bowl, cream butter, sugar, egg, vanilla, and almond extract until light and fluffy. Add flour and mix thoroughly. Divide dough into thirds. Add red and green coloring to two portions of dough. Chill doughs for 1 hour.

Heat oven to 375°. Roll a scant teaspoon of two colors and ½ teaspoon of third color into 4-inch lengths. Place ropes side by side and gently press together. Twist tricolored ropes and lightly roll into one 6-inch rope twisting ends of rope to increase stripes. Place ropes on ungreased cookie sheet; curve the tops down so that they resemble canes. Bake 10 minutes, or until browned on bottom. Carefully remove cookies from sheet; cool on wire rack and sprinkle with sugar while still warm.

Note: Complete cookies one at a time so dough is easily twisted.

Makes about 3½ dozen cookies.

Decorator White Icing

1 package (6 ounces) white
   baking bars, chopped
3 tablespoons heavy cream
¾ cup confectioners' sugar, sifted
3 tablespoons butter *or*
   margarine, softened
¼ teaspoon almond, orange *or*
   mint extract
   Paste colors (optional)

Combine baking bars and heavy cream in top of double boiler, over hot (not boiling) water, stirring until baking bars are melted and mixture is smooth. Remove from heat; transfer to small mixer bowl. Beat in confectioners' sugar, butter, and extract until smooth.

To color icing, use paste colors rather than liquid food color. Spread or pipe icing on favorite sugar cookies. Let stand until set. Refrigerate decorated cookies in single layer.

Makes 1¼ cups frosting.

Simple Sugar Cookies

½ cup shortening
½ cup butter
1 cup granulated sugar
1 egg, beaten slightly
2½ cups all-purpose flour
1 teaspoon almond extract

Preheat oven to 375°. Cream together shortening, butter and sugar. Add beaten egg, mix well. Add flour gradually, blending well. Between palms, roll mixture into small balls and place on lightly greased cookie sheet three inches apart. Dip flat-bottomed glass into dish of sugar and then press bottom against cookie ball. Repeat, dipping bottom of glass into sugar for each cookie. Do not press too thin or cookie will crumble when baked. Bake at 375° for 12 minutes, or until lightly browned. Cookies can be frozen.

Makes 20 to 30 cookies.

Cookie Cutouts

1 cup butter *or* margarine,
   softened
½ cup granulated sugar
½ cup light brown sugar
   (packed)
1 egg
1 teaspoon vanilla extract
3 cups all-purpose flour
1 teaspoon baking soda
   Assorted fruit snacks
   Icing (optional)

In large mixer bowl, cream margarine and sugars until light and fluffy. Beat in egg and vanilla until smooth. Mix flour and baking soda. Gradually add to creamed mixture, blending well after each addition. Chill 2 hours, or until firm.

Heat oven to 375°. Lightly grease cookie sheets. On lightly floured board, roll dough to ⅛-inch thickness; cut into assorted shapes. Decorate with fruit snacks. Place on prepared cookie sheets. Bake 8 to 9 minutes. Cool completely on wire rack. Decorate, if desired, with icing.

Makes 4½ dozen cookies.

Variations

Spicy Cookie Cutouts: Increase brown sugar to ¾ cup and add 1½ teaspoons ground cinnamon and 1 teaspoon ground ginger to flour mixture.

Chocolate Cookie Cutouts: Decrease flour to 2¾ cups, increase granulated sugar to 1 cup and add ½ cup unsweetened cocoa to flour mixture.

Chocolate Raspberry Linzer Cookies

2⅓ cups all-purpose flour
1 teaspoon baking powder
½ teaspoon ground cinnamon
½ teaspoon salt
1 cup granulated sugar
¾ cup butter *or* margarine, softened
2 eggs
½ teaspoon almond extract
1 package (12 ounces) semisweet chocolate pieces
6 tablespoons raspberry jam or preserves
Confectioners' sugar

In small bowl, combine flour, baking powder, cinnamon, and salt; set aside. In large mixer bowl, cream sugar and butter until fluffy. Beat in eggs and almond extract. Gradually add flour mixture. Divide dough in half. Wrap each in plastic wrap and chill until firm, about 3 hours.

Heat oven to 350°. On lightly floured board, roll half of dough to ⅛-inch thickness. Cut with 2½-inch round cookie cutter. Repeat with remaining dough. Cut 1-inch round centers from half of unbaked cookies. Place on ungreased cookie sheets. Reroll dough trimmings. Bake 8 to 10 minutes, or *just* until set. Cool 2 minutes. Remove to wire rack; cool completely.

In top of double boiler, over hot (not boiling) water, melt chocolate pieces, stirring until smooth. Spread 1 measuring teaspoonful chocolate on flat side of each whole cookie. Top with ½ measuring teaspoon raspberry jam. Sprinkle sugar on cookies with center holes; place flat-side down on top of chocolate-jam cookies to form sandwiches.

Makes 3 dozen cookies.

New Wave Chocolate Spritz Cookies

1 package (6 ounces) semisweet chocolate pieces
1 cup butter *or* margarine, softened
⅔ cup granulated sugar
1 teaspoon vanilla extract
2 eggs
2½ cups all-purpose flour
1 jar (4 ounces) cinnamon candies

In top of double boiler, over hot (not boiling) water, melt chocolate pieces, stirring until smooth; set aside.

In large mixer bowl, cream butter, sugar, and vanilla until fluffy. Beat in eggs. Stir in melted chocolate pieces. Gradually beat in flour. Cover dough and chill 30 to 45 minutes.

Heat oven to 400°. Place dough in cookie press fitted with star tip. Press dough into 2-inch circles on ungreased cookie sheets; decorate with cinnamon candies. Bake 5 minutes, or until just set. Cool 2 minutes. Remove to wire rack; cool completely.

Makes 7½ dozen cookies.

Chocolate Mint Pinwheels

1 package (10 ounces) semisweet chocolate mint flavored pieces
¾ cup butter *or* margarine, softened
⅓ cup granulated sugar
½ teaspoon salt
1 egg
1 teaspoon vanilla extract
2¼ cups all-purpose flour

In top of double boiler, over hot (not boiling) water, melt ½ cup mint flavored pieces, stirring until smooth. Cool to room temperature; set aside.

In large mixer bowl, cream butter, sugar, and salt until light and fluffy. Beat in egg and vanilla. *Mixture may look curdled.* Gradually add flour. Place 1 cup dough in bowl; blend in melted chocolate. Shape each dough into a ball; flatten and cover with plastic wrap. Chill until firm, about 1½ hours.

Heat oven to 375°. Between sheets of waxed paper, roll each ball of dough into 13x9 inches. Remove top layer of waxed paper. Invert chocolate dough onto plain dough. Peel off waxed paper. Starting with a long side, roll up, jelly roll style. Cut into ¼-inch slices; place on ungreased cookie sheets.

Bake 7 to 10 minutes. Cool 2 minutes. Remove to wire racks; cool completely.

In top of double boiler, over hot (not boiling) water, melt remaining mint flavored pieces, stirring until smooth. Spread flat side of each cookie with slightly rounded ½ teaspoonful chocolate. Refrigerate 10 minutes to set chocolate.

Makes 4 dozen cookies.

Chocolate Mint Snow-Top Cookies

1½   cups all-purpose flour
1½   teaspoons baking powder
¼   teaspoon salt
1   package (10 ounces) mint
     flavored semisweet
     chocolate pieces
6   tablespoons butter *or*
     margarine, softened
1   cup granulated sugar
1½   teaspoons vanilla extract
2   eggs
     Confectioners' sugar

In small bowl, combine flour, baking powder, and salt; set aside. In top of double boiler, over hot (not boiling) water, melt 1 cup chocolate pieces, stirring until smooth. In large mixer bowl, cream butter and sugar until light and fluffy. Add melted chocolate pieces and vanilla. Beat in eggs. Gradually beat in flour mixture. Stir in remaining ½ cup chocolate pieces. Wrap dough in plastic wrap and freeze until firm, about 20 minutes.

Heat oven to 350°. Shape dough into 1-inch balls; coat with confectioners' sugar. Place on ungreased cookie sheet. Bake 10 to 12 minutes, or until tops appear cracked. Cool 5 minutes. Remove to wire rack; cool completely.

Makes about 3 dozen cookies.

SPECIAL HINT

Microwave chocolate pieces in microwave-safe bowl on HIGH (100% power) 1 minute; stir. Microwave on HIGH 30 seconds longer; stir until smooth.

Moist & Minty Brownies

1¼   cups all-purpose flour
½   teaspoon baking soda
¼   teaspoon salt
¾   cup granulated sugar
½   cup butter *or* margarine
2   tablespoons water
1   package (10 ounces) mint
     flavored semisweet
     chocolate pieces
1   teaspoon vanilla extract
2   eggs

Heat oven to 350°. Grease 9-inch square baking pan. In small bowl, combine flour, baking soda, and salt; set aside. In small saucepan, combine sugar, butter, and water. Bring *just to a boil;* remove from heat. Add 1 cup chocolate pieces and vanilla, stirring until pieces are melted and mixture is smooth. Transfer to large mixer bowl. Add eggs, one at a time, beating well after each addition. Stir in flour mixture and remaining chocolate pieces. Spread in prepared baking pan. Bake 25 to 35 minutes, or just until center is set. Cool completely on wire rack. Cut into 2¼-inch squares.

Makes 16 brownies.

Continental Christmas Breakfast

. . . .

*After Christmas presents are opened and appreciated,
it's time to relax and enjoy breakfast with family and friends.*

Date-Apricot Coffeecake

4 to 4½ cups all-purpose flour
 ⅓ cup granulated sugar
 1 package active dry yeast
 ½ teaspoon salt
 ¾ cup evaporated milk (not
   condensed)
 ⅓ cup butter *or* margarine
 ¼ cup water
 2 eggs, at room temperature
 1 teaspoon vanilla extract
 2 tablespoons apricot preserves
 ½ cup chopped pitted dates,
   snipped
 ½ cup dried apricots, snipped
 ¼ cup chopped pecans, toasted
   (optional)
   Confectioners' Sugar Frosting
   (follows)

In large mixer bowl, combine 1½ cups flour, sugar, yeast, and salt. Heat milk, butter, and water until very warm (120° to 130°). (Butter does not need to melt.) Gradually add to flour mixture; beat 2 minutes at medium speed, scraping bowl occasionally. Add eggs, vanilla, and ½ cup flour; at high speed, beat 2 minutes, scraping bowl occasionally. With spoon, stir in enough additional flour to make soft dough. Knead on lightly floured board until smooth and elastic, about 4 to 5 minutes. Place in greased bowl; turn to grease top. Cover; let rise in warm, draft-free place until doubled in size, about 1 hour.

Grease large cookie sheet. Punch dough down. Roll dough to a 15x12

inch rectangle. Spread apricot preserves to within ½-inch of edges. Evenly sprinkle dates, apricots, and pecans over dough. Roll up from long side as for jelly roll; pinch seam to seal. Set diagonally on prepared cookie sheet. With sharp knife, cut slits, 1½ inches apart, almost through dough. Alternating sides, pull cut pieces out and turn so cut sides face up; lie flat to form two rows of filled rounds. Cover; let rise in warm, draft-free place until doubled in size, about 30 to 40 minutes.

Heat oven to 350°. Bake 25 to 30 minutes, or until golden brown. Remove to wire rack. Cool. If desired, frost with Confectioners' Sugar Frosting.

Makes 1 coffeecake.

Confectioners' Sugar Frosting
 1 cup confectioners' sugar
 4 to 5 teaspoons evaporated
   milk (not condensed)
 ½ teaspoon vanilla extract

In small bowl, combine confectioners' sugar, milk, and vanilla, beating until smooth.

Chocolate Almond Panettone

3½ to 4 cups all-purpose flour
 ⅓ cup granulated sugar
 1 package active dry yeast
 ¾ teaspoon salt

 ¾ cup evaporated milk
   (not condensed)
 ⅓ cup butter *or* margarine
 ¼ cup water
 3 eggs, at room temperature
 ½ cup mini semisweet
   chocolate pieces
 ½ cup chopped blanched
   slivered almonds, toasted

In large mixer bowl, combine 1½ cups flour, sugar, yeast, and salt. In saucepan, heat milk, butter and water until very warm (120° to 130°). Gradually add flour mixture; at medium speed, beat 2 minutes, scraping bowl occasionally. Add 2 eggs and ½ cup flour; at high speed, beat 2 minutes, scraping bowl occasionally. With spoon, stir in enough additional flour to make stiff dough. Cover; let rise in warm, draft-free place until doubled in size, about 1 hour.

Generously grease two 1-pound coffee cans. With spoon, stir dough down; stir in chocolate pieces and almonds. Divide dough in half; place in prepared coffee cans. Cover; let rise in warm, draft-free place until dough rises to within ½ inch of rim, about 40 minutes.

Heat oven to 350°. Beat remaining egg with 1 tablespoon water; brush tops with egg mixture. Bake on lowest oven rack 35 minutes, or until golden brown. Cool in cans on wire rack 5 minutes: turn out onto rack and cool completely.

Makes 2 loaves.

Scandinavian Holiday Bread

- 4 to 4½ cups all-purpose flour
- ½ cup granulated sugar
- 1 package active dry yeast
- 1 teaspoon ground cardamom
- ½ teaspoon salt
- ¾ cup evaporated milk (not condensed)
- ¼ cup water
- ⅓ cup butter *or* margarine
- 3 eggs, at room temperature

In large mixer bowl, combine 1½ cups flour, sugar, yeast, cardamom, and salt. In saucepan, heat milk, water, and butter until very warm (120° to 130°). (Butter does not need to melt.) Gradually add to flour mixture; at medium speed, beat 2 minutes, scraping bowl occasionally. Add 2 eggs and ½ cup flour; beat 2 minutes at high speed, scraping bowl occasionally. With spoon, stir in enough additional flour to make a soft dough. Knead on lightly floured board until smooth and elastic, about 4 minutes. Place in greased bowl, turning to grease top. Cover; let rise in warm, draft-free place until doubled in size, about 1 hour.

Grease large cookie sheet. Punch dough down. Divide dough into 3 equal pieces; roll each to 22-inch rope. Fold one rope in half; place in center of prepared cookie sheet with open end at bottom. Coil ends up, using one-third of dough at each end. Wrap second and third ropes around first rope; coil ends up. Cover; let rise in warm, draft-free place until almost doubled in size, about 45 minutes.

Heat oven to 350°. Lightly beat remaining egg; brush on coffeecake. Bake 35 minutes, or until done, covering with aluminum foil after 20 minutes to prevent excess browning. Remove from cookie sheet; cool on wire rack.

Makes 1 loaf.

Cranberry Wreaths

- 3½ to 4 cups all-purpose flour
- ¼ cup granulated sugar
- 1 package active dry yeast
- 1 teaspoon salt
- ¾ cup evaporated milk (not condensed)
- ¼ cup butter *or* margarine
- ¼ cup water
- 2 eggs, at room temperature
- Cranberry Filling (follows)
- Confectioners' Sugar Frosting (follows)

In large mixer bowl, combine 1½ cups flour, sugar, yeast, and salt. In saucepan, heat milk, butter and water until very warm (120° to 130°). Gradually add to flour mixture; at medium speed, beat 2 minutes, scraping bowl occasionally. Add eggs and ½ cup flour; at high speed, beat 2 minutes, scraping bowl occasionally. With spoon, stir in enough additional flour to make stiff batter. Cover loosely with plastic wrap; chill 2 to 24 hours.

Grease two cookie sheets. Make Cranberry Filling; set aside. Punch dough down. On lightly floured surface, roll dough to 21x12-inch rectangle. Spread entire surface of dough with Filling. Fold ⅓ of dough over from narrow side. Fold remaining section of dough over, making a 12x7-inch rectangle. Press edges to seal. Cut dough into 12 one-inch strips. Holding ends of each strip, twist in opposite directions three times. Pinch ends of each twisted strip to form wreaths. Place on prepared cookie sheets. Cover; let rise in warm, draft-free place until almost doubled in size, about 30 minutes.

Bake 12 to 15 minutes, or until golden brown. Remove from cookie sheets; cool on wire rack. If desired, frost with Confectioners' Sugar Frosting.

Makes 12 wreaths.

Cranberry Filling

- 1 cup finely chopped cranberries
- ½ cup granulated sugar
- 1½ teaspoons grated orange zest

In saucepan, combine ingredients. Bring to boil over medium heat and cook, stirring, 5 minutes. Cool.

Confectioners' Sugar Frosting

- 1 cup confectioners' sugar
- 4 to 5 teaspoons evaporated milk (not condensed)
- ½ teaspoon vanilla extract

In small bowl, combine ingredients, beating until smooth.

Raisin Cinnamon Rolls

- 1 loaf (1 pound) frozen bread dough, thawed
- ½ cup butter *or* margarine, melted
- ½ cup granulated sugar
- 2 teaspoons ground cinnamon
- ½ cup raisins
- 2 tablespoons chopped almonds, toasted
- 2 teaspoons grated lemon zest
- ½ cup confectioners' sugar
- 2 teaspoons lemon juice

Grease 9-inch pie plate or baking pan. Roll thawed dough on floured board to 14x8 inches. Reserve 2 tablespoons butter; brush remaining butter over dough. Combine sugar and cinnamon; sprinkle over dough along with raisins, almonds and lemon zest. Starting from long side, roll up jelly roll style. Cut into 12 pieces. Arrange in prepared pie plate or baking pan.

At this point, allow dough to rise in refrigerator overnight, or heat oven to 350°. Brush with reserved 2 tablespoons butter. Bake 30 minutes. Cool 10 minutes. To serve, combine confectioners' sugar and lemon juice until smooth. Brush glaze over rolls.

Makes 12 rolls.

Winter's Secrets

There are sounds in the sky when the
    year grows old,
And the winds of the winter blow —
When night and the moon are clear and cold,
And the stars shine on the snow;
Or wild is the blast and the bitter sleet
That beats on the window pane.
But blest on the frosty hills are the feet
Of the Christmas time again!
Chiming sweet when the night wind swells,
Blest is the sound of the Christmas Bells!

AUTHOR UNKNOWN

Christmas Turkey Dinner

*Crisp roast turkey is always a welcome treat on Christmas Day.
Creamy Carrot Soup is a soothing start to a wonderful meal. And, for dessert,
the Maple Pumpkin Pie will surely please everyone's palate.*

Creamy Carrot Soup

½ cup chopped onion
1 clove garlic, finely chopped
2 tablespoons butter *or* margarine
5 cups water
2 pounds carrots, pared and sliced
2 medium tomatoes, seeded and chopped (2 cups)
5 teaspoons chicken bouillon
¼ cup lemon juice
1 teaspoon dried leaf basil, crumbled
⅛ teaspoon black pepper
1 cup half-and-half *or* milk

In large kettle or Dutch oven, cook onion and garlic in butter until tender. Add water. Stir in carrots, tomatoes, bouillon, lemon juice, basil, and pepper. Bring to boil. Reduce heat; cover and simmer until carrots are tender. In blender or food processor, purée half the carrot mixture. Transfer to large saucepan. Repeat with remaining mixture. Over low heat, stir in half-and-half; cook and stir until hot. Serve hot, or cover and chill.

Makes 10 to 12 servings.

Cornbread-Pecan Stuffing

1 cup chopped celery
1 cup chopped green bell pepper
1 cup chopped onion
1½ teaspoons poultry seasoning
¼ teaspoon ground sage
½ cup butter or margarine
1 tablespoon chicken bouillon
2 cups boiling water
1 package (16 ounces) cornbread stuffing mix
1 cup chopped pecans
2 eggs, slightly beaten

Heat oven to 350°. Grease baking dish. In large skillet, sauté celery, green pepper, onion, poultry seasoning, and sage in butter until tender. In large bowl, dissolve bouillon in water. Add celery mixture, stuffing mix, pecans, and eggs; mix well. Loosely stuff turkey just before roasting. Place remaining stuffing in prepared baking dish. Bake stuffing 30 minutes, or until hot.

Makes about 8 cups (enough to stuff a 10- to 12-pound turkey).

Roast Turkey

10-12 pound turkey, fresh or frozen

Follow directions on package for thawing frozen turkey. Wash turkey and pat dry. Remove neck and giblets. Rub cavity lightly with salt and/or half lemon. (Do not salt if turkey is to be stuffed.)

Cook giblets in 4 cups water to make stock for gravy; reserve. Stuff turkey with stuffing and fasten with skewers.

Heat oven to 325°. Place turkey, breast side up, on rack in open shallow roasting pan. Brush with oil, butter, or shortening. Insert meat thermometer into breast or thickest part of thigh muscle. Roast until thermometer registers 185°. Cover drumsticks and breast with foil or cheesecloth when it starts to brown.

When turkey is done, remove and allow to stand about 20 minutes. Remove stuffing as soon as possible.

Makes 10 to 12 servings.

Rich Turkey Gravy

¼ to ⅓ cup all-purpose flour
¼ cup turkey pan drippings
2 cups boiling water
2 teaspoons chicken bouillon

In medium skillet stir flour into drippings over medium heat; cook and stir until dark brown. Stir in water and bouillon; cook and stir until thickened and bouillon is dissolved.

Makes about 1½ cups.

Savory Cranberry Stuffing

1 cup chopped celery
1 cup chopped onion
½ cup butter *or* margarine
1 can (16 ounces) whole berry cranberry sauce
2 tablespoons chicken bouillon
12 cups dry bread cubes (about 16 slices)
1 cup chopped pecans
2 teaspoons poultry seasoning
1 teaspoon ground sage
3 cups hot water

Heat oven to 350°. Grease baking dish. In large skillet, sauté celery and onion in butter until tender. In small saucepan cook and stir cranberry sauce and bouillon over low heat until bouillon dissolves. In large bowl, combine bread cubes, pecans, poultry seasoning, sage, and water. Add celery and cranberry mixtures. Mix well. Loosely stuff turkey just before roasting. Place remaining stuffing in prepared baking dish. Bake stuffing 30 minutes, or until hot.

Makes about 10 cups (enough to stuff a 12- to 14-pound turkey).

Pistachio-Apricot Stuffing

¼ cup butter *or* margarine
1 cup water
¾ cup apricot nectar
1 package (7 ounces) herb-seasoned stuffing mix
1 cup pistachios
1 cup chopped onion
½ cup chopped dried apricots
½ cup chopped pitted dates

Heat oven to 350°. Grease baking dish. In large saucepan, combine butter, water, and apricot nectar. Cook over low heat until butter is melted. Stir in stuffing mix until well moistened. Mix in pistachios, onions, apricots, and dates. Loosely stuff turkey just before roasting. Place remaining stuffing in prepared baking dish. Bake stuffing 1 hour, or until hot.

Makes about 6 cups (enough to stuff a 10- to 12-pound turkey).

Maple Acorn Squash

2 acorn squash, cut horizontally into ½-inch rings, seeds and membrane removed (about 2½ pounds)
½ cup water
1 cup maple syrup
2 tablespoons butter *or* margarine, melted
1 tablespoon cornstarch
2 teaspoons grated orange zest
½ teaspoon ground cinnamon
¼ teaspoon ground nutmeg

Heat oven to 350°. Place squash and water in 15x10-inch jelly roll pan; cover with aluminum foil. Bake 35 minutes; drain. Combine maple syrup, butter, cornstarch, orange zest, cinnamon, and nutmeg; brush squash with syrup mixture. Bake, uncovered, 25 minutes, basting often with syrup mixture.

Makes 6 to 8 servings.

Maple Pumpkin Pie

1 can (16 ounces) solid pack pumpkin
1 cup half-and-half
3 eggs, slightly beaten
½ cup plus 2 tablespoons maple syrup
⅓ cup light brown sugar (packed)
1 teaspoon ground cinnamon
½ teaspoon ground ginger
½ teaspoon ground nutmeg
1 9-inch unbaked pastry shell
Maple Whipped Cream (follows)

Heat oven to 425°. In large mixer bowl, combine pumpkin, half-and-half, eggs, ½ cup syrup, sugar, cinnamon, ginger, and nutmeg; mix well. Pour into pastry shell. Bake 15 minutes. Reduce oven temperature to 350°; bake 25 to 30 minutes longer, or until knife inserted near edge comes out clean. Cool; brush with remaining 2 tablespoons syrup. Serve with Maple Whipped Cream.

Makes one 9-inch pie.

Maple Whipped Cream

1 cup heavy cream
¼ cup maple syrup

In small mixer bowl, beat cream and maple syrup until stiff.

Makes about 2 cups.

Apricot-Walnut Mince Pie

- 1 package (6 ounces) dried apricots
- 1 jar (27 ounces) ready-to-use mincemeat
- 1 cup chopped walnuts
- 1 9-inch unbaked pastry shell
- 1 container (16 ounces) sour cream, at room temperature
- 1 tablespoon granulated sugar
- 1 teaspoon vanilla extract

Heat oven to 400°; place oven rack in lowest position. Chop ½ cup apricots; reserve remainder. In medium bowl, combine mincemeat, chopped apricots, and walnuts; turn into pastry shell. Bake 25 minutes.

Meanwhile, in medium bowl, combine sour cream, sugar, and vanilla. Spread evenly over pie. Bake 8 minutes longer, or until set. Cool. Garnish with reserved apricots.

Makes one 9-inch pie.

Cratchet's Christmas Pudding

- ⅔ cup chopped suet
- ⅔ cup chopped candied orange peel
- ¼ cup chopped candied lemon peel
- 1½ cups raisins
- 1 cup chopped figs
- 2 cups graham cracker crumbs
- 1 tablespoon ground cinnamon
- 1½ teaspoons ground ginger
- ½ teaspoon ground allspice
- ¼ teaspoon ground nutmeg
- 1 teaspoon salt
- 1 cup granulated sugar
- 1 can (8¼ ounces) crushed pineapple
- ⅓ cup raspberry preserves
- 4 eggs
- ¾ cup brandy
  Almond Cream Sauce (follows)

Generously grease 2-quart pudding mold or 9-cup Bundt pan. In large bowl, combine suet with peels, raisins, figs, crumbs, cinnamon, ginger, allspice, nutmeg, salt, and sugar. Blend undrained pineapple with raspberry preserves. Stir into fruit mixture. Beat eggs. Stir in ½ cup brandy. Fold into fruit just until blended. Turn into prepared mold. Cover tightly. (If Bundt pan is used, press foil firmly into outer edges and around center hole to cover completely.) Place on rack in large kettle. Pour boiling water into pan to come halfway up mold. Cover; steam 4 hours. (Water should be gently boiling.) Remove from water. Cool 5 minutes. Invert onto serving platter and remove mold. In small saucepan heat ¼ cup brandy over medium heat.

Ignite with wooden match; pour over pudding. Serve warm with Almond Cream Sauce.

Makes 12 servings.

Almond Cream Sauce

- 1 package (4-serving size) vanilla pudding and pie filling mix (not instant)
- ½ teaspoon almond extract
- 1 cup heavy cream
- 1 cup milk
- ¼ cup brandy

In saucepan, combine pudding mix, almond extract, cream, and milk. Heat to boiling, stirring. Remove from heat; stir in brandy. Serve warm, or cover and chill. Just before serving, beat until smooth and creamy.

Makes 2½ cups.

Simply Festive

· ·

Serve these luscious and easy-to-make recipes for easy entertaining.

Cranberry-Glazed Chef's Prime

2 to 4 pound boneless pork rib-end roast
2 teaspoons cornstarch
⅛ teaspoon ground cinnamon
⅛ teaspoon salt
4 tablespoons orange juice
1 can (16 ounces) whole cranberry sauce

In small saucepan, combine cornstarch, cinnamon, and salt. Stir in orange juice and cranberry sauce. Cook, stirring, over medium heat until thickened; set aside.

Heat oven to 325°. Place roast in shallow roasting pan and spoon over about ½ cup cranberry sauce. Roast 45 minutes to 1 hour, basting occasionally with additional sauce, or until meat thermometer reads 155-160°. Remove from oven. Let stand 10 minutes before carving. Serve with additional cranberry sauce.

Makes 8 servings.

Wild Rice Salad

1 cup wild rice
2½ cups chicken broth
3 tablespoons vegetable oil
2 tablespoons red wine vinegar
2 tablespoons minced green onion (white part only)
1½ teaspoons Dijon mustard
¼ teaspoon black pepper
1 small green pepper, seeded and diced

In large heavy saucepan, bring rice and broth to a boil. Reduce heat; cover and simmer 45 to 50 minutes until *just* tender. Drain; cool to room temperature. Combine oil, vinegar, onion, mustard, black pepper, and green pepper; toss with rice. Cover and refrigerate. Serve at room temperature.

Makes 6 to 8 servings.

SPECIAL HINTS

To prepare orange pieces: Cut off peel of oranges round and round, spiral fashion. Go over fruit again, removing any remaining white membrane. Cut along the side of each dividing membrane from outside to middle of core. Remove section by section over bowl to retain juice; cut sections in thirds.

Orange Eggnog Pie

1 package (3 ounces) ladyfingers
1 envelope unflavored gelatin
½ cup granulated sugar
⅛ teaspoon salt
1 cup orange juice
2 tablespoons rum
½ teaspoon grated orange zest
2 egg whites
1 cup orange pieces

To prepare crust, split ladyfingers and cut one end off enough ladyfingers to stand, crust-side out, around side of 9-inch pie plate. Arrange remaining ladyfingers and ends, crust-side down, over the bottom of the pie plate.

In medium saucepan, mix gelatin, ¼ cup sugar, and salt. Stir in ½ cup orange juice. Place over medium heat; stir constantly until gelatin dissolves, about 5 minutes. Remove from heat; stir in remaining ½ cup orange juice, rum, and orange zest.

Chill, stirring occasionally, until mixture mounds slightly when dropped from a spoon. In mixer bowl, beat egg whites until soft peaks form. Gradually beat in remaining ¼ cup sugar; beat until stiff peaks form. Fold into gelatin mixture; fold in orange pieces. Turn into prepared crust. Chill until set. To serve, garnish with orange sections.

Makes 8 servings.

Orange Date Steamed Pudding

- ½ cup polyunsaturated margarine
- 2 teaspoons grated orange zest
- 1 cup dark brown sugar (packed)
- ½ cup cholesterol-free egg substitute
- 1¼ cups sifted all-purpose flour
- 2½ teaspoons baking powder
- ½ teaspoon salt
- ¼ teaspoon baking soda
- ½ teaspoon ground nutmeg
- ½ cup orange juice
- 2 tablespoons brandy
- ½ cup chopped pitted dates
- ½ cup chopped walnuts
- ¼ cup unsifted all-purpose flour
  Orange Sauce (follows)

Grease and sugar 6-cup pudding mold. In large mixer bowl, cream margarine, orange zest, and sugar until fluffy. Beat in egg substitute. Sift 1¼ cups flour, baking powder, salt, baking soda, and nutmeg; add flour mixture to creamed mixture, alternately with orange juice and brandy. Mix dates and walnuts with remaining ¼ cup flour. Stir into batter. Turn into prepared molds. Cover and place on rack in large kettle. Add water to come halfway up sides of mold. Tightly cover kettle. Bring to a boil, reduce heat, and simmer 2½ hours, or until cake tester inserted in center of mold comes out clean. Remove mold from water. Uncover mold. Cool 10 minutes. Unmold onto serving dish. Cut into wedges and serve with Orange Sauce.

Makes 10 to 12 servings.

Orange Sauce

- ½ cup granulated sugar
- 2 tablespoons cornstarch
- ⅛ teaspoon salt
- 1 cup water
- ¼ cup orange juice
- 2 tablespoons cholesterol-free egg substitute
- 2 cups orange sections
- ½ teaspoon grated orange zest

In medium saucepan, mix sugar, cornstarch, and salt. Stir in water. Cook over medium heat, stirring constantly, until mixture thickens and comes to boil. Mix orange juice and egg substitute; stir in a little hot mixture. Stir into saucepan. Heat but do not boil. Remove from heat; stir in sections and orange zest.

SPECIAL HINTS

The steamed pudding may be prepared ahead and reheated just before serving. Wrap in foil and heat in 350° oven 30 minutes.

To section oranges: Cut slice from top, then cut off peel in strips from top to bottom, cutting deep enough to remove white membrane. Then cut slice from bottom. Or cut off peel round and round, spiral fashion. Go over fruit again, removing any remaining white membrane. Cut along the side of each dividing membrane from outside to middle of core. Remove section by section over bowl.

Welcome Friends Buffet

An extravagant array of tasty dishes — and a wonderful way to be a guest at your own party. Set everything out on an attractively decorated table and exchange holiday greetings with friends and neighbors.

Orange Mustard Glazed Ham

- 1 5-pound boneless fully cooked ham
- 1 can (6 ounces) frozen concentrate for orange juice, thawed
- ⅓ cup spicy brown mustard
- 2 tablespoons Worcestershire sauce

Heat oven to 325°. In shallow roasting pan, bake ham, uncovered, 15 minutes. Score top of ham in diamonds or squares. In small bowl, combine orange juice concentrate, mustard, and Worcestershire sauce; mix well. Brush ham with orange-mustard sauce. Bake 1 hour longer, brushing often. Remove from oven and let stand 5 minutes before slicing. Serve with remaining orange-mustard sauce.

Makes 20 servings.

Orange Cream Extravaganza

- 2 envelopes unflavored gelatin
- 4 cups orange juice
- 2 cups vanilla ice cream, softened
- ¼ cup hazelnut-flavored liqueur
- 1 cup heavy cream, whipped
- 2 oranges, sectioned
  Chopped hazelnuts

In medium saucepan, combine gelatin and 1 cup orange juice; let stand 1 minute. Stir over medium heat until gelatin is completely dissolved. Add remaining 3 cups orange juice; mix well. Pour mixture into bowl and chill until slightly thickened. Stir in ice cream and liqueur until mixture is smooth. Spoon into individual serving dishes or 6-cup serving bowl. Chill 8 hours, or overnight. To serve, garnish with whipped cream, orange sections, and hazelnuts.

Makes 12 servings.

Marinated Grapefruit Salad

- 2 cups thinly sliced fennel
- 2 jars (7 ounces each) roasted peppers, cut in pieces
- 1 can (12 ounces) artichoke hearts, drained and halved
- 1 medium red onion, thinly sliced
- ¼ cup bottled Italian salad dressing
- ½ cup grapefruit juice
- ¼ teaspoon ground fennel seeds
- 3 grapefruits, sectioned

In large bowl, combine fennel, peppers, artichokes, onion, dressing, juice, and fennel seeds; mix well. Chill 3 to 4 hours to blend flavors; stirring occasionally. (Recipe can be prepared day before to this point.) Just before serving, stir in grapefruit sections.

Makes 12 servings.

International Sausage Medley

- 2 pounds mixed sausages (veal, beef, pork), cut in 1-inch pieces
- 1 tablespoon vegetable oil (optional)
- 1½ cups sliced onions
- 2 cloves garlic, minced
- 2 cups grapefruit juice
- ¼ cup light brown sugar (packed)
- 3 tablespoons cider vinegar
- ⅛ teaspoon hot pepper sauce
- 1 tablespoon cornstarch
- 2 grapefruits, sectioned

In large skillet, cook sausages 10 to 15 minutes, or until browned on all sides. Remove sausages; set aside. Add oil to skillet if necessary. Sauté onions and garlic 2 minutes, scraping up browned bits from bottom of pan. Add 1¾ cups grapefruit juice, sugar, vinegar, and pepper sauce; stir until sugar is dissolved. Return sausages to skillet; baste with pan liquid. Simmer, covered, 15 minutes, or until sausages are cooked through, basting often. Combine remaining ¼ cup grapefruit juice and cornstarch. Add to skillet, stirring constantly until mixture boils and thickens. (Recipe can be prepared to this point the day before.) Add grapefruit sections; heat through.

Makes 12 appetizer servings.

Mexican Appetizer Cheesecake

2 teaspoons chicken
   bouillon
½ cup *hot* water
3 packages (8 ounces each)
   cream cheese, softened
1½ teaspoons chili powder
½ to 1 teaspoon hot pepper sauce
2 eggs
1 cup finely chopped
   cooked chicken
1 can (4 ounces) chopped
   green chilies, *well
   drained*
   Salsa, shredded cheese,
      and sliced green onions
   Tortilla chips

Heat oven to 325°. In small bowl, dissolve bouillon in water; set aside. In large mixer bowl, beat cream cheese, chili powder, and pepper sauce until smooth. Add eggs; mix well. Add bouillon liquid, beating until smooth. Stir in chicken and chilies. Pour into 9-inch springform pan. Bake 30 minutes, or until set; cool 15 minutes. Carefully run knife around edge of pan; remove side of pan. Top with salsa, cheese, and onions. Serve warm or chilled with tortilla chips.

Makes 8 to 10 servings.

Clam 'n' Curry Roll-Ups

2 cans (6½ ounces each)
   minced clams, drained
½ cup mayonnaise
1 tablespoon grated onion
¼ to ½ teaspoon curry powder
8 slices white sandwich
   bread, crusts removed
   Butter *or* margarine,
      melted
   Chopped parsley or
      toasted sesame seeds
      (optional)

In small bowl, combine clams, mayonnaise, onion, and curry powder. Using a rolling pin, flatten each bread slice. Spread 2 tablespoons clam mixture on each; roll up. Brush with butter. Wrap in plastic wrap; refrigerate or freeze until firm.

Heat oven to 450°. Roll in chopped parsley, if desired. Cut each roll into 4 pieces; place on rack in shallow baking pan. Bake 8 to 10 minutes, or until golden brown. Serve immediately.

Makes 32 appetizers.

Herb Clam Spread

2 packages (8 ounces each)
   cream cheese, softened
½ cup butter *or* margarine
2 cans (6½ ounces each)
   chopped clams, drained,
   reserving 2 tablespoons
   liquid
1 teaspoon dried leaf oregano,
   crumbled
¼ teaspoon dried leaf basil,
   crumbled
¼ teaspoon dried leaf marjoram,
   crumbled
¼ teaspoon dried leaf thyme,
   crumbled
¼ teaspoon dill weed
¼ teaspoon garlic powder
   Assorted crackers and fresh
      vegetables

In large mixer bowl, beat cream cheese and butter until fluffy. Add reserved 2 tablespoons clam liquid, oregano, basil, marjoram, thyme, dill, and garlic powder; mix well. Stir in clams. Cover; chill to blend flavors, at least 2 hours. Spoon into crock. Serve with crackers and vegetables.

Makes 3½ cups.

Marinated Pork Orientale

½ cup lemon juice
¼ cup light brown sugar
   (packed)
¼ cup orange juice
¼ cup soy sauce
⅓ cup vegetable oil
⅓ cup sliced green onions
1 tablespoon finely chopped
   fresh ginger *or* ¾ teaspoon
   ground ginger
2 pork tenderloins
   (about ¾ pound each)
1 cup peach *or* apricot preserves
   French bread, thinly sliced
   Thinly sliced jicama, fresh pea
      pods, and red bell pepper
      strips

In blender container or small mixer bowl, combine lemon juice, sugar, orange juice, and soy sauce; blend well. On low speed, continue blending, slowly adding oil. Remove ¼ cup soy mixture; set aside. Combine onions and ginger with remaining soy mixture; pour over tenderloins in glass dish. Cover; marinate in refrigerator 4 hours, or overnight. In small saucepan, combine reserved ¼ cup soy mixture and preserves. Over low heat, cook and stir until preserves melt. Cover; chill. Heat oven to 450°. Drain and reserve marinade. Arrange tenderloins on rack in aluminum foil-lined baking pan. Bake 10 minutes. Reduce oven temperature to 350°; bake 25 to 30 minutes longer, or until meat thermometer reaches 155°, basting frequently with marinade. Cover; chill. Serve thinly sliced tenderloins with sauce, bread, jicama, pea pods and peppers.

Makes 10 appetizer servings.

Red Caviar Mousse Spread

- 1 envelope unflavored gelatin
- ½ cup bottled clam juice
- 1 container (8 ounces) sour cream
- ¼ cup chopped shallots *or* onion
- 1 tablespoon lemon juice
- 1 teaspoon Dijon mustard
- ½ teaspoon paprika
- ⅛ teaspoon pepper
- 1 cup whipping *or* heavy cream
- 1 jar (2 ounces) red caviar
  Toast points
  Hard-cooked egg, chopped
  Lemon slices (optional)

In small saucepan, sprinkle gelatin over clam juice; let stand 1 minute. Stir over low heat 3 minutes, or until gelatin is completely dissolved.

In blender or food processor, process sour cream, shallots, lemon juice, mustard, paprika, and pepper. Gradually add gelatin mixture, then cream; process 15 seconds. Pour into 4-cup mold or bowl; stir in caviar. Chill 3 hours, or until firm. Unmold and serve with toast points and egg.

Makes 3½ cups.

Tuscan Meatballs

- 3 cloves garlic, peeled
- 1 pound ground round steak
- 1 baking potato, peeled, cooked, and diced
- 2 eggs
- ½ cup freshly grated Parmesan cheese
- ¼ cup chopped parsley
- 1 tablespoon dried leaf sage, crumbled
- ¼ teaspoon dried leaf marjoram, crumbled
- 2 tablespoons lemon juice
  Salt and pepper to taste
- 60 medium mushrooms, stems removed
- ½ cup dry bread crumbs
- ¼ cup butter *or* margarine, melted (optional)
  Coarsely chopped parsley

In food processor fitted with metal blade, drop in garlic; process until minced. Add beef and process until finely chopped. Add potato, eggs, cheese, parsley, sage, margarine, lemon juice, salt, and pepper. Mix until well-blended. Place in pastry bag with no tip. Place mushroom caps open side up on ungreased cookie sheets. Pipe beef mixture into mushroom caps. Sprinkle balls with bread crumbs. Chill 2 hours, or until firm. Heat oven to 500°. If desired, drizzle tops with melted butter. Bake 7 minutes, or until set. Garnish each with parsley.

Makes 5 dozen.

SPECIAL HINTS

Meatballs can be frozen for 1 week. To freeze: Form meatballs, place in single layer on waxed paper, and freeze until firm. Transfer to airtight container. To serve, thaw meatballs in refrigerator overnight. Place meatballs in mushroom caps; proceed as directed.

Chinese-Style Dumplings

1 pound ground round steak
6 water chestnuts, diced (fresh, if possible; peel first)
2 green onions, finely chopped
1 carrot, peeled and grated
1 tablespoon grated orange zest
1 egg
¼ cup Chinese plum sauce
1 tablespoon cornstarch
1 tablespoon soy sauce
1½ teaspoons Chinese chili paste with garlic *or* 2 cloves minced garlic and dash of red pepper
1 package (1 pound) small wonton wrappers

In food processor fitted with plastic blade, place beef, water chestnuts, onions, carrot, orange zest, egg, plum sauce, cornstarch, soy sauce, and chili paste. Process until well blended. Work with about 6 wrappers at a time, keeping remaining wrappers covered. Place 1 tablespoon beef mixture in center of each wrapper. Bring edges of wrapper up around filling. Pinch sides into tiny pleats. Flatten bottom of dumpling. Place each dumpling on a lightly greased dish that will fit in a bamboo steaming basket. Chill until ready to cook.

Bring water to boil in bottom of wok. Set steamer basket in wok and place plate of dumplings in steamer basket; cover and steam over medium-high heat 10 minutes. Serve hot directly from basket.

Makes 42 dumplings.

Argentine Meat Pies

¼ cup chopped onion
¼ cup chopped red bell pepper
1 cup water
1 pound ground round steak
¼ cup raisins, soaked in boiling water until plump
½ teaspoon red pepper flakes
½ teaspoon paprika
¼ teaspoon ground cumin
Salt and pepper to taste
Pastry Dough (follows)
Sliced pitted green olives

In skillet, heat onion, bell pepper, and water to boiling. Simmer until water has evaporated. Add beef; cook and stir until browned. Add raisins, chili flakes, paprika, cumin, salt, and pepper; set aside. Heat oven to 400°. Prepare Pastry Dough. On floured board, roll out pastry dough to ⅛-inch thickness. Cut into 3-inch circles. Place 1 teaspoon filling on each circle. Top with a few slices of olives. Moisten edges of circles; fold over and press edges to seal. Pinch edges to form a rope-like shape. Place on ungreased cookie sheet. Bake 10 minutes, or until lightly browned.

Makes 3 dozen appetizers.

Pastry Dough
3 cups all-purpose flour
1 cup butter *or* margarine, cut into bits
1½ teaspoons salt
½ cup cold water

In large bowl, mix flour, butter and salt. With pastry blender or 2 forks, blend mixture until it resembles coarse meal. Sprinkle with water; gather into a ball.

White Fruit Tart

Pastry for 9-inch pie shell
¼ cup apricot jam, melted
⅓ cup granulated sugar
⅓ cup all-purpose flour
1 cup milk
3 egg yolks
1 package (6 ounces) white baking bars, chopped
1 teaspoon vanilla extract
White Chocolate Leaves (follows)
2 kiwifruit, peeled and sliced
¼ cup fresh raspberries

Heat oven to 425°. Line 9-inch loose-bottom tart pan with pastry; trim edges. With fork, prick pastry in several places. Bake 10 to 12 minutes, or until crust is lightly browned. Cool on wire rack. Brush pastry with melted jam; set aside.

In medium saucepan, combine sugar and flour; gradually whisk in milk and egg yolks. Cook over medium heat, stirring constantly, until mixture boils. Reduce heat and cook, whisking constantly, 3 minutes, or until mixture is thickened and smooth. Remove from heat; stir in baking bars and vanilla until smooth. Pour mixture into tart shell; press plastic wrap directly on surface and chill 30 minutes.

Remove tart from pan. Make White Chocolate Leaves and arrange with raspberries on top of tart. Chill until ready to serve.

Makes 6 to 8 servings.

White Chocolate Leaves

Wash and *dry very well* about 6 non-toxic leaves, such as lemon leaves, grape leaves, rose leaves, violet leaves or nasturtium leaves; set aside. In saucepan, melt 4 ounces white baking bars or white deluxe baking pieces. Onto the back side of each leaf, spoon or brush melted mixture about ¹⁄₁₆-inch.

If mixture runs over edge of leaf, wipe off edge of leaf with fingertip. Place coated leaves on plate or cookie sheet; chill 30 minutes, or until firm. Gently peel leaf from firm white chocolate mixture. Arrange leaves on dessert.

Makes about 6 large leaves.

Fresh Fruit Fruitcake

½ cup unsalted butter, cut up
¼ cup heavy cream
2½ cups cake flour
2 teaspoons baking powder
1 teaspoon salt
3 eggs, at room temperature
1¼ cups granulated sugar
4 medium, ripe pears, peeled, cored, and cut into 1-inch chunks
½ cup coarsely chopped walnuts
2 cups fresh or frozen cranberries (do not thaw)
Lightly sweetened whipped cream
Poached Cranberries in Syrup (follows)

Heat oven to 350°. Grease 10x3 inch cake *or* springform pan. Line bottom of pan with circle of waxed paper; grease paper.

In small saucepan, heat butter and cream over low heat, stirring, until butter melts; set aside. Sift cake flour, baking powder, and salt; set aside.

In large mixer bowl, beat eggs and sugar on high speed 5 minutes, or until pale yellow and fluffy. On low speed, gradually beat in half the flour mixture, ½ cup at a time, mixing thoroughly after each addition. Pour in half the warm butter mixture and beat until blended. Add remaining flour mixture, ½ cup at a time, then remaining butter mixture. Scrape down side of bowl. On medium-high speed, beat 2 minutes, or until mixture is thickened. Using a rubber spatula, fold in pears and nuts. Add the cranberries. (There will be only enough batter to lightly coat fruit.) Scrape batter into prepared pan.

Bake on center rack 1 hour 15 minutes, or until top is golden brown, and cake tester inserted in center comes out clean. Remove from oven and cool in pan on wire rack 20 minutes. Remove cake from pan and peel off waxed paper. Invert cake on wire rack to cool completely. Serve with whipped cream and Poached Cranberries in Syrup.

Makes 16 servings.

Poached Cranberries in Syrup

1 cup granulated sugar
1 cup water
1 package (12 ounces) fresh *or* frozen cranberries (do not thaw)

In medium noncorrodible saucepan, combine sugar with water. Bring to boil over moderate heat, stirring to dissolve sugar. Turn heat off and add cranberries; stir gently. Remove from heat; let berries cool in syrup. Drain.

Coconutty Butter Balls

½ cup butter *or* margarine, softened
2 tablespoons confectioners' sugar
½ teaspoon vanilla extract
1 cup all-purpose flour
1⅓ cups flaked coconut

In large mixer bowl, beat butter until light and fluffy. Mix in sugar and vanilla. Stir in flour until well blended. Stir in ⅔ cup of coconut. Chill 15 minutes.

Heat oven to 350°. Shape into 1-inch balls. Roll in remaining coconut and bake on ungreased cookie sheets 15 minutes, or until lightly browned. Cool.

Makes 3 dozen cookies.

Christmas Log

Chocolate Sponge Roll (follows)
Mocha Whipped Topping (follows)
Chocolate Glaze (follows)
2 tablespoons chopped pistachios *or* almonds
Candied cherries, halved or quartered

Make Chocolate Sponge Roll; cool. Make Mocha Whipped Topping; fill cake roll with topping. Roll and place on serving platter. Make Chocolate Glaze spread over top and sides of cake roll; sprinkle with chopped nuts and decorate with cherry pieces. Refrigerate until serving time.

Makes 10 to 12 servings.

Chocolate Sponge Roll

⅔ cup all-purpose flour
½ teaspoon baking powder
½ teaspoon salt
5 eggs, at room temperature
¾ cup granulated sugar
2 or 2½ squares (2 or 2½ ounces) unsweetened chocolate
¼ cup cold water
2 tablespoons granulated sugar
¼ teaspoon baking soda
Confectioners' sugar

Heat oven to 350° Grease bottom and sides of 15x10-inch jelly roll pan; line with waxed paper; grease paper.

In small bowl, mix flour, baking powder and salt. In large bowl, beat eggs at high speed, gradually adding sugar. Beat until mixture is fluffy, thick, and light in color. Gradually fold in flour mixture.

In small saucepan, melt chocolate over low heat; immediately add cold water, 2 tablespoons sugar, and baking soda, stirring until thick and smooth. Stir quickly into batter. Pour into prepared pan. Bake 20 minutes, or until cake tester inserted in center comes out clean.

Turn out onto cloth, which has been sprinkled lightly with confectioners' sugar. Quickly remove paper and trim off crisp edges of cake. Starting with narrow side, roll up cake, rolling cloth with cake. Cool on wire rack. Unroll, spread with desired filling, and roll up again, placing seam-side down. Sprinkle with additional confectioners' sugar, or spread with Chocolate Glaze. (If a cream filling is used, store in refrigerator.)

> ### SPECIAL HINT
>
> At high altitudes, bake at 375° for 13 to 18 minutes.

Mocha Whipped Topping

½ cup cold milk
¼ cup granulated sugar
1 tablespoon instant coffee powder
1 tablespoon unsweetened cocoa
½ teaspoon vanilla extract
1 envelope whipped topping mix

In deep narrow-bottom mixer bowl, combine milk, sugar, coffee, cocoa, vanilla, and topping mix. Beat at high speed until topping peaks. Continue beating 2 minutes, or until topping is light and fluffy.

Makes 2 cups.

Chocolate Glaze

1 square (1 ounce) unsweetened chocolate
1 tablespoon butter or margarine
¾ cup confectioners' sugar
Dash of salt
2 tablespoons hot milk

In small saucepan, melt chocolate with butter over very low heat. Remove from heat. Add sugar and salt, alternately with milk, a small amount at a time, until mixture is of glaze consistency. Spread glaze while still warm.

Makes ½ cup.

Variation: Melt chocolate in 1-quart microwave-safe bowl on HIGH (100% power) 1 minute; stir until smooth. Add butter and microwave 20 seconds.

Easy Chocolate Cheesecake

Crumb Crust (follows)
2 packages (4 ounces each)
   sweet chocolate
2 eggs
⅔ cup light *or* dark corn syrup
⅓ cup heavy cream
1½ teaspoons vanilla extract
2 packages (8 ounces each)
   cream cheese, cut in cubes
   and softened

Make Crumb Crust; set aside. In microwave-safe dish, heat 1½ packages (6 ounces) chocolate on HIGH (100% power) 1½ to 2 minutes, until almost melted, stirring once. Stir until smooth; set aside.

Heat oven to 325°. In blender, blend eggs, corn syrup, cream, and vanilla until smooth. With blender running, gradually add cream cheese; blend until smooth. Blend in chocolate. Pour into crust. Bake 45 minutes, or until set. Cool on wire rack. Cover; chill. Melt remaining chocolate; drizzle over top.

Makes 8 servings.

Crumb Crust
1¾ cups chocolate cookie *or*
   graham cracker crumbs
2 tablespoons granulated sugar
⅓ cup butter *or* margarine,
   melted

In 9-inch pie plate or 9x3-inch springform pan, combine crumbs, sugar, and butter until well mixed. Press evenly in pie plate or on bottom and 1¼ inches up side of springform pan.

Chocolate Eggnog Pie

1 package (4 ounces) sweet
   chocolate
⅓ cup milk
2 tablespoons granulated sugar
1 package (3 ounces) cream
   cheese, softened
2 eggs, separated
2 tablespoons rum *or* 2
   teaspoons rum flavoring
1 container (4 ounces) non-
   dairy whipped topping,
   thawed
¼ cup chopped toasted almonds
1 baked 9-inch graham cracker
   crumb crust, cooled
Non-dairy whipped topping
   (optional)
Chopped toasted almonds
   (optional)
Chocolate curls (optional)

In small saucepan, heat chocolate and 2 tablespoons of milk over low heat; stir until chocolate is melted. In large mixer bowl, beat sugar into cream cheese; add egg yolks and blend well. Add chocolate mixture, rum, and remaining milk; beat until smooth.

In small mixer bowl, beat egg whites until stiff but not dry; fold into chocolate mixture. Fold in whipped topping, blending well. Add almonds. Spoon into crust. Freeze 4 hours, or until firm. Garnish with additional whipped topping and nuts and/or chocolate curls, if desired.

Lacy Chocolate Crisps

½ cup light corn syrup
⅓ cup butter *or* margarine
1 package (4 ounces) sweet
   chocolate
½ cup light brown sugar
   (packed)
1 cup all-purpose flour
⅔ cup flaked coconut

Heat oven to 300°. Lightly grease two cookie sheets. In saucepan, bring corn syrup to boil. Add butter and chocolate; cook and stir over low heat until chocolate is melted and mixture is smooth. Remove from heat; stir in sugar, flour, and coconut. Drop from tablespoon 3 inches apart onto prepared cookie sheets. Bake 15 minutes, or until wafers are bubbling vigorously and have developed lacy holes throughout. Cool 2 minutes. Using a thin spatula, carefully remove. (If wafers become too difficult to remove, return to oven for a minute or two.) Cool completely on wire rack.

Makes about 30 large wafers.

SPECIAL HINTS

Cookies may be shaped over aluminum foil cones or rolled over handle of wooden spoon while still warm. Fill with ice cream or prepared whipped topping.

Fruit Medley Punch

  **Della Robbia Ice Ring,
    optional**
2 **(10 ounces) packages frozen
    strawberries in syrup,
    partially thawed**
3 **cups apricot nectar, chilled**
3 **cups cold water**
1 **cup lemon juice**
1 **(6 ounces) can frozen orange
    juice concentrate, thawed**
1 **cup sugar**
1 **(32 ounces) bottle ginger ale,
    chilled**

Prepare ice ring in advance. In blender container, blend strawberries well. In punch bowl, combine puréed strawberries, apricot nectar, water, lemon juice, orange juice concentrate and sugar; stir until sugar dissolves. Slowly pour in ginger ale; add Della Robbia Ice Ring, if desired.

Makes about 3½ quarts.

Della Robbia Ice Ring

2½ **cups ginger ale, chilled**
  ½ **cup lemon juice**
    **Canned apricot halves,
      drained**
    Seedless green grapes
    **Strawberries *or* maraschino
      cherries**
    Strips of orange zest, curled
    Mint leaves

In 1-quart measure or pitcher, combine ginger ale and lemon juice. Pour 2 cups into 1-quart ring mold; freeze solid. Arrange apricots, grapes, strawberries, orange zest, and mint in mold. Carefully pour remaining liquid over fruit in mold. Freeze solid. Unmold and float in punch bowl.

Champagne Sherbet Punch

3 **cups pineapple juice, chilled**
¼ **cup lemon juice**
1 **quart pineapple sherbet**
1 **bottle (750 ml) champagne,
    chilled**

In punch bowl, combine pineapple and lemon juice. Just before serving, scoop sherbet into punch bowl; add champagne. Stir gently.

Makes about 2½ quarts.

Welcoming New Year

Wonder and Promise

Sending New Year's cards had its heyday in the early part of this century...and sending cards is still a modern-day way of celebrating the welcome future. The old year has ended and we want to acknowledge a beautiful new year that holds wonder and promise. Prosperity, abundance and good luck can be ours. The past has faded away and we can look forward to a renewed life—or so it seems.

Every important new beginning needs a formal ritual that says good-bye to whatever is over and done with. Today's New Year's Eve party is a ritual that "sees out" the old year and "sees in" the new. We can all celebrate our awareness and our vision. It's the time to reaffirm our faith in a new year that will bring happiness and good luck.

Traditionally, the old year and the spirits of blight and pestilence were driven out of the community so that everyone could have a new lease on life. An image of Death—sometimes made of braided hemp and straw, and dressed in old clothes—was carried through the village in a procession. Then the effigy was either burned, buried or drowned in a stream. Good riddance to bad rubbish!

What's Lucky...and What Isn't

Folklore and superstitions that predict the future for celebrants is varied and interesting. New Year's Day is thought to be auspicious, because whatever happens on that day foretells what will happen in the coming year. That's why it's necessary to abide by certain rules. Do the right things and avoid the wrong ones.

What will ensure good fortune? The ancient Romans wore white on January 1st. In other times, everyone dressed in new clothes. Since "clothes makyth man", clothes were thought to be a symbol of character and individuality. Accordingly, at New Year, a new identity could be assumed for each person and for the community as a whole.

There was another reason for a change of clothing. New garments provided an easy disguise and protected the wearer from the many demons and evil spirits who were thought to be wandering about at year's end. The idea was that you could avoid harm by not being recognized. This disguise aspect is a forerunner of our present custom of wearing masks on New Year's Eve and taking them off at the stroke of midnight.

If a change of clothes is the right thing to do at New Year, what should you avoid? Well, for one, don't keep a borrowed item in the house over New Year's Day. If you do, you'll be dependent on others for the next twelve months.

Next, no household member should leave the house and no household goods should be brought outside—and that included garbage, ashes or dirty water. The traditional English rhyme says:

> *Take out and then take in*
> *Bad luck will begin;*
> *Take in and then take out,*
> *Good luck comes about.*

The fireplace fire and the table lamp represent "warmth" and "light". When they burn brightly—folklore tells us—they assure continuance of the family and all that it symbolizes. So, it's not surprising that people avoided extinguishing candles or carrying other lights outside the house at New Year.

Other superstitions compelled people to make sure that their pockets and cupboards were not empty on New Year's Day. Otherwise, pockets and cupboards would stay empty throughout the coming year.

"Be careful about breaking glasswear," people thought. "It means other things will also be damaged in the next twelve months. And avoid starting lawsuits—for New Year is a time for people of the community to reaffirm their connection to one and other."

Precious Portents

Of course, everyone wants to know what's in store for him or her in the year ahead. There have been a lot of diverse and intriguing ways to learn the future.

In Germany and England, "scrying" on New Year's Day meant that a householder poured molten metal into a bowl of water. When the metal formed shapes in the water, the seer "read" the shapes and made predictions — in much the same way that tea leaves left in the bottom of a cup can be "read."

Or, if you didn't happen to have any molten metal around the house, you could read fireplace ashes from the New Year's Eve celebration. In Scotland, it was thought that if the coals were still glowing at daybreak, the family's good fortune was assured for the entire

year. But, if the fire had died out, it was surely a bad omen.

Still more New Year omens could be divined from the ashes. Seeing the shape of a human foot with toes pointing toward the door meant that a family member was going to leave the household. If the toes pointed away from the door, a new family member could be expected.

Where else could people look to find omens? Fortune-seekers looked into the heavens to find their fate. Good weather on New Year's Day (and throughout January) meant that good weather could be anticipated until May. An Old English rhyme informs us:

If the Calends of January may be smiling & gay,
You'll have wintry weather till the Calends of May.

155

Or, first thing on New Year's morning, people could look out the window for an animal. But take note! If its head is turned towards you and the animal is standing, you'll have good luck. If its tail is towards you and he's lying down—the coming year will bring adversity.

Perhaps many people have heard that—on New Year's Day—it's lucky if the person you meet is carrying packages. If the person is empty-handed, it's supposed to be unlucky. And it doesn't bode well to meet a cat or dog before you meet a human.

What about the first person who crosses the threshold in the New Year? That special someone is called a "first-footer". If he or she was born feet first—a breech birth—then extra-good fortune will come along.

Sometimes a first-footer was just a family member that went outside and then came in again. To greet the New Year and spread good luck throughout the house, he or she tossed grain everywhere, as a symbol of fertility and abundance.

Generosity of Spirit

New Year's gifts have almost always been symbols of rebirth. Ancient Persians gave gifts of eggs. Early Britons gave gifts of mistletoe, also called "all-heal", and thought to be a cure-all for many illnesses. In other times, apples, nuts and oranges were given to represent fruitfulness. Today, we send New Year's cards with verses that also send good luck and happiness to the recipient.

The generous New Year feast reaffirms ties of friendship and kinship. What is eaten in *communitas* at this time ensures that friends, family and neighbors have re-established their loving bonds...and will continue to do so in the New Year.

The wassail bowl can be simmering with apples and spices. Glasses can be raised high and many clever toasts can be given. In the nineteenth century, at midnight on New Year's Eve, revelers danced around the table and sang:

Our wassail do we fill
With apples and with spice:
The grant us your good will
To taste here once or twice
Of our good wassail.

Today we express sentiments such as "love and joy come to you"...even though we no longer sing them.

Auld Lang Syne and New Year's Resolutions

Robert Burns, the Scottish poet wrote *Auld Lang Syne*, the song that we all enjoy singing on New Year's Eve. The words "Should auld acquaintance be forgot, and never brought to mind..." is a beautiful reminder of the loving friendships we continue to cherish over the years.

After festivities, the first day of the year also reminds us that we have new plans to make and new promises to keep, especially to ourselves. Four thousand years ago, ancient Babylonians made resolutions to pay off outstanding debts and to return borrowed household utensils and farming tools. Today resolutions are very often geared toward keeping a healthy diet and exercising...and to spending all our time more fruitfully. On the bright New Year, it seems easy to break old habits and begin life again more productively.

Rejoice In Noisemaking and In Solitude

Janus is the Roman god that represents January. His name is derived from "janua", which means "door". He is always shown with two faces—one looks backward, and the other looks forward. The faces of Janus show us that the past and the future are contained in the present creative moment. The process of creation is continuous—and the world is reborn again and again, from year to year.

Rejoice...and bring about new beginnings! What happened in the past is over. And the future has not yet arrived. Glory in New Year's Eve, the stroke of midnight...and the newborn Baby who brings new life and hope to the world.

After the Eve's partying, New Year's Day can be a time of quietly rekindling hopes and dreams in thoughtful solitude. Rejoice in peaceful contemplation and the wonderful future that is yours!

Dina von Zweck

New Year's Day Feast

· ·

*A steaming Wassail Bowl and Rolled Lamb Roast
set the mood for a sumptuous and simple-to-make
New Year's Day feast.*

Rolled Lamb Roast with Spinach Crème Fraîche

- 1 boned, rolled and tied leg of lamb (5 pounds)
- ¼ cup vegetable oil
- 1 teaspoon salt
- ½ teaspoon pepper
- 1 teaspoon dried leaf rosemary, crumbled
- 2 cloves garlic, cut into slivers
- 2 tablespoons butter *or* margarine
- ¼ cup minced shallots *or* onion
- 1 cup chopped mushrooms
- 12 ounces fresh spinach leaves, washed and trimmed (about 5 cups)
- ½ cup chicken stock *or* broth
- ½ teaspoon ground nutmeg
- ¼ cup Spinach Crème Fraîche
- 1 tablespoon cornstarch
- 2 tablespoons water
- 1 teaspoon lime juice
  Salt and pepper to taste

Heat oven to 325°. Rub lamb roast with oil, salt, pepper and rosemary.

Cut ¼-inch slits on top of roast; insert garlic slivers. Place lamb on rack of broiler pan. Roast 2 hours, or until thermometer inserted into thickest portion registers 140° for rare, or 150-155° for medium-rare.

Meanwhile, in large skillet, melt butter. Add shallots and mushrooms and sauté until soft. Add spinach and chicken stock; cover and heat until wilted. Remove from heat. Stir in nutmeg, and salt and pepper to taste. Pour into food processor or blender; process until puréed. Return mixture to pan; add crème fraîche. Dissolve cornstarch in 2 tablespoons water. Add to spinach mixture; stir over medium heat until smooth and thickened. Stir in lime juice. Adjust seasonings, if desired.

To serve, slice lamb and place over Spinach Crème Fraîche.

Makes 10 servings.

Golden Apples and Yams

- 2 large yams
- 2 Golden Delicious apples, cored and sliced crosswise
- ¼ cup light brown sugar (packed)
- 1 teaspoon cornstarch
- ⅛ teaspoon ground cloves
- ½ cup orange juice
- 2 tablespoons chopped pecans *or* walnuts

Heat oven to 400°. Bake yams 50 minutes, or until slightly soft but still firm. Peel and slice crosswise. Reduce oven temperature to 375°. Overlap apples and yams in shallow 1-quart baking dish. In small saucepan, combine sugar, cornstarch, and cloves. Add orange juice and blend. Heat until syrupy; pour over apples and yams. Sprinkle with nuts. Bake 20 minutes, or until apples and yams are tender.

Makes 6 servings.

Steamed Pear-Cranberry Pudding

	1	to 2 ripe pears
	1	cup halved cranberries
	1½	cups all-purpose flour
	2	teaspoons baking soda
	½	teaspoon salt
	½	cup hot water
	½	cup molasses
		Butter Sauce (follows)

Grease 6-cup mold. In small bowl, core and dice pears to equal 1 cup. Combine with cranberries. In large bowl, sift flour, baking soda, and salt. Add fruit and mix well. In small bowl, combine hot water with molasses and stir into flour mixture. Pour into prepared mold, filling only ⅔ full to allow for expansion during cooking. Cover with lid or greased aluminum foil. Place on rack in deep kettle. Add boiling water to come halfway up side of mold. Cover and simmer 2 hours, or until wooden pick inserted in center comes out clean. Cool mold on wire rack 10 minutes. Loosen pudding and invert onto serving platter. Serve warm or cold with Butter Sauce.

Makes 6 to 8 servings.

Butter Sauce

	6	tablespoons butter or
		margarine
	¾	cup granulated sugar
	6	tablespoons half-and-half

In small saucepan, combine butter, sugar, and half-and-half. Cook and stir until sugar is dissolved.

Makes about 1 cup.

Twelfth Night Cake

	2½	cups all-purpose flour
	1	teaspoon baking soda
	1	teaspoon salt
	½	teaspoon ground cinnamon
	¾	cup butter or margarine
	1¾	cups granulated sugar
	¾	cups orange juice
	½	cup milk
	2	eggs
	2	tablespoons grated orange
		zest
	1	teaspoon vanilla extract
	½	cup chopped walnuts
	½	cup golden raisins
	¼	cup currants
	1	whole blanched almond

Heat oven to 350°. Generously grease Bundt or 10-inch tube pan. In large bowl, sift flour, baking soda, salt, and cinnamon. In large mixer bowl, cream butter and 1½ cups sugar, until light and fluffy. Add ½ cup orange juice, milk, eggs, orange zest, and vanilla. Gradually add flour mixture, beating until combined. Fold in walnuts, raisins, currants, and whole almond. Turn into prepared pan. Bake 55 minutes, or until cake tester inserted in center comes out clean. Cool 15 minutes in pan.

In a small saucepan, heat 1 cup cream to between 90° and 100°. Pour into a small bowl. Stir in ¼ slightly. Prick surface of cake with a fork. Slowly pour orange mixture over cake in pan. Cool completely in pan. Remove from pan. Cake is best if allowed to stand overnight before slicing.

Makes 12 to 16 servings.

Wassail Bowl

	1	cup granulated sugar
	½	cup light brown sugar
		(packed)
	4	cups apple cider
	1	cinnamon stick
		(about 3 inches)
	12	whole cloves
	2	cups grapefruit juice
	2	cups orange juice
		Orange slices
		Halved maraschino cherries
		Whole cloves

In large saucepan, combine sugars, and apple cider; cook and stir until sugar dissolves. Add cinnamon stick and cloves. Bring mixture to boil over medium heat; reduce heat and simmer 5 minutes. Add juices. Heat, but do not boil. Strain. Serve in heatproof mugs with orange slices decorated with maraschino cherry halves and whole cloves.

Makes 8 servings.

The More You Give

Give strength, give thought, give deeds, give wealth;
Give love, give tears, and give thyself.
Give, give, be always giving.
Who gives not is not living;
The more you give, the more you live.

AUTHOR UNKNOWN

Christmastime
MEMORIES
1991

Christmas Wish List

For family gift ideas

What _____ wants for Christmas _____

_____

_____

_____

_____

What _____ wants for Christmas _____

_____

_____

_____

_____

What _____ wants for Christmas _____

_____

_____

_____

_____

What _____ wants for Christmas _____

_____

_____

_____

_____

What _____ wants for Christmas _____

_____

_____

_____

_____

What _____ wants for Christmas _____

_____

_____

_____

_____

What _____ wants for Christmas _____

_____

_____

_____

_____

What _____ wants for Christmas _____

_____

_____

_____

_____

What _____ wants for Christmas _____

_____

_____

_____

_____

What _____ wants for Christmas _____

_____

_____

_____

_____

Favorite Christmas Memories

Christmas Cards

Cards Sent _____

_____

_____

_____

_____

_____

_____

_____

_____

_____

_____

_____

_____

_____

Cards Received _____

_____

_____

_____

_____

_____

_____

_____

_____

_____

_____

_____

_____

_____

Cards Sent _____

_____

_____

_____

_____

_____

_____

_____

_____

_____

_____

Cards Received _____

_____

_____

_____

_____

_____

_____

_____

_____

_____

_____

_____

_____

Seasonal Family Activities

Special outings and activities during the holidays

Holiday Get-Togethers

For remembering when we got together with family and friends

Where We Got Together _____

What We Did _____

_____

_____

_____

_____

_____

_____

_____

_____

_____

_____

_____

Where We Got Together _____

What We Did _____

_____

_____

_____

_____

_____

_____

_____

_____

_____

_____

Where We Got Together _____

What We Did _____

_____

_____

_____

_____

_____

_____

_____

_____

_____

_____

Where We Got Together _____

What We Did _____

_____

_____

_____

_____

_____

_____

_____

_____

_____

_____

_____

Telephone Calls

Calls Made

_____
_____
_____
_____
_____
_____
_____
_____
_____
_____
_____
_____
_____
_____
_____
_____
_____
_____
_____
_____
_____
_____
_____
_____
_____
_____
_____

Calls Received

_____
_____
_____
_____
_____
_____
_____
_____
_____
_____
_____
_____
_____
_____
_____
_____
_____
_____
_____
_____
_____
_____
_____
_____
_____

Christmas Gifts

Gifts Given

_____

_____

_____

_____

_____

_____

_____

_____

_____

_____

_____

_____

_____

_____

_____

_____

_____

_____

_____

_____

_____

_____

_____

_____

_____

_____

_____

_____

Gifts Received

_____
_____
_____
_____
_____
_____
_____
_____
_____
_____
_____
_____
_____
_____
_____
_____
_____
_____
_____
_____
_____
_____
_____

How We Spent the Holidays

Christmas Eve

Where We Celebrated _____

How We Celebrated _____

_____

_____

_____

_____

_____

_____

_____

_____

_____

_____

_____

_____

_____

_____

_____

_____

_____

_____

_____

_____

_____

_____

_____

_____

_____

_____

_____

Christmas Day

Where We Celebrated _____

How We Celebrated _____

_____

_____

_____

_____

_____

_____

_____

_____

_____

_____

_____

_____

_____

_____

_____

_____

_____

_____

_____

_____

_____

_____

_____

_____

_____

How We Spent the Holidays

New Year's Eve   New Year's Day

Where We Celebrated _____

How We Celebrated _____

_____

_____

_____

_____

_____

_____

_____

_____

_____

_____

_____

Where We Celebrated _____

How We Celebrated _____

_____

_____

_____

_____

_____

_____

_____

_____

_____

_____

_____

_____

Holiday Favorites

Stories, Carols, Movies, TV Shows, Poems, Books

_____

_____

_____

_____

_____

_____

_____

_____

_____

_____

_____

_____

_____

_____

_____

_____

_____

_____

_____

_____

_____

_____

_____

_____

_____

_____

_____

New Holiday Traditions

Recipes, Decorations, Activities

_____
_____
_____
_____
_____
_____
_____
_____
_____
_____
_____
_____
_____
_____
_____
_____
_____
_____
_____
_____
_____
_____
_____
_____
_____
_____
_____
_____
_____
_____
_____

Special Moments to Treasure

Photos and other holiday memorabilia

Special Moments to Treasure

Photos and other holiday memorabilia

Special Moments to Treasure

Photos and other holiday memorabilia

HOLIDAY
DATEBOOK
1991

Thursday 28	■ **Thanksgiving Day** (United States)

Friday 29	

Saturday 30	

Sunday 1	

Monday 2	

Tuesday 3	

Wednesday 4	

Thursday

5

Friday

6

Saturday

7

Sunday

8

Monday

9

Tuesday

10

Wednesday

11

Thursday

12

Friday

13

Saturday

14

Sunday

15

Monday

16

Tuesday

17

Wednesday

18

Thursday

19

Friday

20

Saturday

21

Sunday

22

Monday

23

Tuesday   ■ Christmas Eve

24

Wednesday **25**	■ Christmas Day
Thursday **26**	■ Boxing Day (Canada)
Friday **27**	
Saturday **28**	
Sunday **29**	
Monday **30**	
Tuesday **31**	JANUARY
Wednesday **1**	■ New Year's Day

Acknowledgements

· ·

CREDITS
pp. 90 Christmas card reprinted with permission from Hallmark Cards, Inc.
pp. 49, 55, 69, 87, 92, 95. Background Fabric, Laura Ashley
pp. 67, 90. Background Fabric, Marimekko
Background Christmas decorations and wrappings, Hallmark Cards, Inc.

The publisher would like to thank those who generously granted permission for use of the following:

TEXT
"Meet Me In The City" by Van Varner. Reprinted with permission from Daily Guideposts, 1990. Copyright © 1984 by Guideposts Associates, Inc. Carmel, New York 10512.
"Christmas Closes A Gulf" from ACT ONE: AN AUTOBIOGRAPHY by Moss Hart. Copyright © 1959 by Catharine Carlisle Hart & Joseph M. Hyman, Trustees. Reprinted with permission of Random House, Inc.
"The Christmas Day Heart" by Dean Collins from WHITE CROWN SINGING. Copyright © by Margaret E. Ballard.
"An Exchange of Gifts" by Diane Rayner. Reprinted with permission from Guideposts Magazine. Copyright © 1983 by Guideposts Associates, Inc. Carmel, New York 10512.
"One Room, One Window" by Eva Dunbar. Reprinted with permission from Guideposts Magazine. Copyright © 1967 by Guideposts Associates, Inc. Carmel, New York 10512.
"Hold Fast Your Dreams" by Annette Victorin. Copyright © Annette Victorin.
"The Christmas Ships" by Steven Goldsberry. Reprinted with permission from ALOHA, THE MAGAZINE OF HAWAI'I AND THE PACIFIC.
"Undelivered Gifts" by Wayne Montgomery. Reprinted with permission from Guideposts Magazine. Copyright © 1967 by Guideposts Associations, Inc. Carmel, New York 10512.

ILLUSTRATIONS
pp. Title Page, 13, 76, 78, 161 Copyright © 1991 by Jeanette Martone.
pp. 17–21, 28–29 Copyright © 1991 by Cathy O'Connor.
pp. 24, 34, 46, 99 Copyright © 1991 by Michael Furuya.
pp. 60–61, 74 Copyright © 1991 by Sanford Mock.
p. 37 Illustration by Kenny Kiernan. Copyright © 1991 by Inkwell, Inc.

PHOTOGRAPHS
p. 8 Bethlehem, Pa., Chamber of Commerce.
p. 8 (lower left) © William Clark, photographer. Used by permission of National Park Service, National Capital Region.
p. 8 (lower left) Used by permission of Salt Lake Convention and Visitors Bureau.
pp. 3, 16, 22–23, 53, 134–135, 160 Copyright © John Shaw, photographer. Used by permission of John Shaw.

pp. 4, 7, 14–15, 120–121, Copyright © Ulrich Ruchti, photographer. Used by permission of Ulrich Ruchti.
pp. 4, 5, 27, 97 Copyright © Michael W. Thomas, photographer. Used by permission of Michael W. Thomas.
p. 10 Copyright © Jim Turner, photographer. Used by permission of Jim Turner.
pp. 11 (top) Storrowton Village Museum, Eastern States Exposition.
p. 11 (bottom) Copyright © Frank Guido, photographer. Used by permission of Frank Guido.
p. 12 Minden Chamber of Commerce.
pp. 31, 39, 49, 55, 67, 69, 155 Copyright © Schecter Lee, photographer. Used by permission of Schecter Lee.
p. 42 Robert H. Epstein, photographer. Copyright © 1986 by CBS Magazines, a Division of CBS Inc. Used by permission of Woman's Day magazine.
p. 81 José, photographer.

CRAFTS
pp. 30–33 Trumpeting Angel; Marina Grant, designer.
pp. 38–40 Jingle Bell Wreath; Linda Hebert, designer.
pp. 41–45 Christmas Tree Centerpiece; from SWEET DREAMS OF GINGERBREAD by Jann Johnson Copyright © 1986 by CBS Magazines, a division of CBS Inc., published by Sedgewood® Press, a division of Meredith Corporation.
pp. 48–52 Felt Ornaments; Diane Wagner, designer.
pp. 54–59 Cross-Stitch Angel Ornaments; Pam Bono, designer.
pp. 62–65 Doughcraft Ornaments from AN OLD-FASHIONED CHRISTMAS by Diana Mansour Copyright © Marshall Cavendish 1988, published by Sedgewood® Press, a division of Meredith Corporation.
p. 66–67 Angel Dough Ornament; Diane Wagner, designer.
pp. 68–69 Paper Ribbon Angels; Sydne Matus, designer.
pp. 70–73 Nöel Stocking from AN OLD-FASHIONED CHRISTMAS by Diana Mansour Copyright © Marshall Cavendish Limited 1988, published by Sedgewood® Press, a division of Meredith Corporation.
pp. 80–85 "Picture Pretty" Pinafore Bib; Margaret Boyles, designer.
pp. 86–89 Susannah Dolly; Colette Wolff, designer.
pp. 90–91 Snowy Day Helmet; Karen Buckholz, designer.
pp. 92–93 Sewing Circle Bag; Cheri Tamm Raymond, designer.
pp. 94–95 "Antique" Trinket Box; Hope Eastman, designer.

RECIPES
pp. 100–101 Photo and recipes: Chocolate-Raspberry Mini Cakes; Chocolate Caramels; Favorite Bittersweet Chocolate Sauce. Courtesy of Hershey's® Cocoa.
pp. 102–103 Photo and recipes: Chocolate Almond Biçotti; Holiday Shortbread Cookies; Triple Decker Fudge; Chocolate Chip Candy Cookie Bars. Recipes developed by Hershey Kitchens and provided courtesy of Hershey Foods Corporation.

p. 104 Recipe: Plum Pudding Candy. Courtesy of Sun-Diamond Growers of California.

p. 104 Recipe: No-Bake Fudge. Courtesy of Watkins.

pp. 104–107 Photo and recipes: Chocolate Mint Truffles; Sparkly Cookie Stars; Black Forest Brownies; Harvest Fruit Conserve; Curried Rice Mix; Maple Custard Sauce; Southern-Style Coating Mix; Maple Barbecue Sauce; Herbed Cheese Logs; Three-Bean Soup Mix. Provided by Borden Kitchens, Borden, Inc.

p. 107 Recipe: Orange Fruitcake Bars. Courtesy of Florida Department of Citrus.

p. 107 Recipe: Orange Popcorn Balls. Courtesy of Sunkist Growers, Inc.

pp. 108–109 Photo and recipes: Orange Macaroon Bars; Candied Orange Slices; Orange Chocolate Balls. Courtesy of Florida Department of Citrus.

pp. 109–110 Photo and recipes: Fabulous Orange Fudge; 1000 Palms Stuffed Dates; Western Golden Fruitcake; Candied Citrus Peel; White Citrus Fudge. Courtesy of Sunkist Growers, Inc.

p. 112 Recipe: Teddy Bear Gift Bread. Courtesy of The Sugar Association, Inc.

pp. 112–113 Photos and recipes: Spiced Banana Cookie Wreath; Mandarin Orange Yogurt Tart; Fresh Fruit Tray. Courtesy of Dole®.

pp. 114–115 Photo and recipes: Glazed Pound Cake; Gelatin Poke Cake; Marzipan. Courtesy of General Foods USA.

p. 116 Photo and recipes: Cranberry Walnut Crescents; Cranberry Apple Tea. Provided by Ocean Spray Cranberries, Inc.

p. 117 Photo and recipes: Cranberry Nut Roll; Hot White Chocolate. Courtesy of Nestlé Foods Corporation.

p. 118 Photo and recipe: Pumpkin Cheesecake Bavarian. Courtesy of California Milk Advisory Board.

p. 118 Recipe: Pistachio Truffle Pie. Compliments of California Pistachio Commission.

p. 119 Photo and recipes: Season's Greeting Punch; Raspberry Melody Punch; Hot Orchard Peach Cup; Hot Pineapple Port Cup; Paradise Fruit Nog. Courtesy of Dole®.

p. 119 Recipes: Hot Orange Cranberry Punch; Fireside Punch. Courtesy of Thomas J. Lipton, Inc.

pp. 122–124 Photo and recipes: Chocolate Cherry-Nut Drops; Filled Slice 'N Bake Chocolate Cookies; Cocoa Sandies; Chocolate Pecan Pie Bars; Almond Orange Dainties. Courtesy of Hershey's® Cocoa.

pp. 124–125 Photo and recipe; Christmas Stained Glass Cookies. Courtesy of The Sugar Association.

p. 125 Recipe: Christmas Candy Cane Cookies. Provided by White Satin Sugar.

pp. 126–127 Photo and recipe: Cookie Cutouts. Courtesy of Thomas J. Lipton, Inc.

p. 126 Recipe: Simple Sugar Cookies. Courtesy of The Sugar Association.

pp. 125–130 Photos and recipes: Lemon Nut Cookies; Decorator White Icing; Chocolate Raspberry Linzer Cookies; New Wave Chocolate Spritz Cookies; Chocolate Mint Pinwheels; Chocolate Mint Snow-Top Cookies; Moist and Minty Brownies. Courtesy of Nestlé Foods Corporation.

p. 131–133 Photo and recipes: Date-Apricot Coffeecake; Chocolate

Almond Panettone; Scandinavian Holiday Bread; Cranberry Wreaths. Courtesy of Fleishmann's Yeast.

p. 133 Recipe: Raisin Cinnamon Rolls. Courtesy of Dole®.

pp. 136–139 Photo and recipes: Creamy Carrot Soup; Rich Turkey Gravy; Cornbread-Pecan Stuffing; Savory Cranberry Stuffing; Maple Acorn Squash; Maple Pumpkin Pie; Apricot-Walnut Mince Pie. Courtesy of Borden Kitchens, Borden, Inc.

p. 138 Recipe: Pistachio-Apricot Stuffing. Compliments of California Pistachio Commission.

p. 139 Photo and recipe: Cratchet's Christmas Pudding. Courtesy of Dole®.

pp. 140–141 Photo and recipes: Cranberry-Glazed Chef's Prime; Wild Rice Salad. Courtesy of National Pork Producers Council.

pp. 140–143 Photo and recipes: Orange Eggnog Pie; Orange Date Steamed Pudding; Orange Sauce; Orange Mustard Glazed Ham; Orange Cream Extravaganza; Marinated Grapefruit Salad; International Sausage Medley. Courtesy of Florida Department of Citrus.

pp. 144–145 Photo and recipes: Mexican Appetizer Cheesecake; Clam 'N' Curry Roll-Ups; Herb Clam Spread; Marinated Pork Orientale. Courtesy of Borden Kitchens, Borden, Inc.

p. 146 Photo and recipe: Red Caviar Mousse Spread. Courtesy of Thomas J. Lipton, Inc.

pp. 146–147 Photo and recipes: Tuscan Meatballs; Chinese-Style Dumplings; Argentine Meat Pies. Courtesy of California Beef Council.

p. 148 Photo and recipe: White Fruit Tart; White Chocolate Leaves. Courtesy of Nestlé Foods Corporation.

p. 149 Photo and recipe: Fresh Fruit Fruitcake. Provided by Ocean Spray Cranberries, Inc.

pp. 150–152 Photo and recipes: Coconutty Butter Balls; Christmas Log; Chocolate Sponge Roll; Mocha Whipped Topping; Chocolate Glaze; Easy Chocolate Cheesecake; Chocolate Eggnog Pie; Lacy Chocolate Crisps. Courtesy of General Foods USA.

p. 153 Photo and recipes: Fruit Medley Punch; Della Robbia Ice Ring; Champagne Sherbet Punch. Courtesy of ReaLemon Brand® Lemon Juice, product of Borden, Inc.

pp. 157–158 Photo and recipe: Rolled Lamb Roast With Spinach Crème Fraîche. Compliments of American Lamb Council.

p. 158 Photo and recipe: Golden Apples and Yams. Compliments of Washington Apple Commission.

p. 159 Recipe: Steamed Pear-Cranberry Pudding. Provided by Oregon-Washington-California Pear Bureau.

p. 159 Recipes: Twelfth Night Cake; Wassail Bowl. Courtesy of Florida Department of Citrus.

SPECIAL THANKS TO THE FOLLOWING:

Vangie Sweitzer, Bethlehem, PA., Chamber of Commerce.
Janet S. Weaver, Crossroads Village.
Catherine Pappas, Eastern States Exposition.
Renee Hershey and Sherry Timbrook, Hallmark Cards, Inc.
Marjorie Madsen, Minden Chamber of Commerce.
Mary L. Baldwin, Shreveport—Bossier Convention and Tourist Bureau.
D. J. Arnold, South Dakota Tourism.
Sheryl Harris, Salt Lake Convention & Visitors Bureau.

Index

....